Memories of a Sporting Man

To Martin

Best Wishes

John Waterhouse

JOHN WATERHOUSE

Memories of a Sporting Man

John and Sandra Waterhouse

I wish to thank Sandra for her continued support not only in the production of this book but also in coping with the problems in everyday life due to the fact that I have Parkinson's Disease. At times, her patience is tested.

After enjoying a short break in Blackpool with her mother and our elder daughter Karen – yes, three generations – she arrived home to find that I had painted alternate panels in the wooden facia of the garage a bright blue colour thereby creating the blue and white stripes of Huddersfield Town. Sandra was not very happy but fortunately for me, Karen thought it was a good idea.

This may explain to some readers the design of the front cover.

John Waterhouse

If you wish to order further copies of this publication, please send a cheque for £14.99 (this includes a £2 charge for postage and packing) made payable to J Waterhouse to:

Mr J Waterhouse
6 North Field Way
Appleton Roebuck
York YO23 7EA

email: johnwaterhouse872@btinternet.com

or order it online at www.ypd-books.com

Published by John Waterhouse

ISBN 978-0-9564362-0-7

Cover design by Clare Brayshaw

Prepared and printed by:

York Publishing Services Ltd
64 Hallfield Road
Layerthorpe
York YO31 7ZQ
Tel: 01904 431213

Website: www.yps-publishing.co.uk

Contents

Acknowledgements

I wish to express my thanks to all those who have helped me in the production of this book:

The compilers of the history of Huddersfield Town – 99 Years and Counting.
Harry Lister – Farnley AFC

Paul Fletcher MBE – Burnley FC

George Binns – Huddersfield Town Gentlemens' Sporting Club

David Addinall – Golf

Eric Vevers – statistics and newspaper cuttings for Pudsey Britannia CC

Howard Clayton – Airedale and Wharfedale Senior Cricket League

John Tubby – Leeds Cricket League

Mike and Chris Furze – Bolton Percy CC

Martin Pears (On behalf of his late father Geoff Pears) – Bolton Percy CC

Nigel Thornton, Brian Claughton and Raymond Illingworth – Farsley CC

Mike Rhodes – Bradford Cricket League

Bill Carter, Tony Haines, Keith Houlston, Albert Pattison and Ray Dowdall – York and District Senior Cricket League.

Jack Kell – Menston CC

Derek Boorman and Ian Hillman – Tyke Petroleum Men's Tennis League

Quentin Howat, Marilyn Almgill Ian Connolly and friends – Appleton Roebuck Tennis Club

Marjorie Harrison – for expertise and encouragement.

Gordon and Lorna Bradley for practical assistance.
John Giles – Photography

Daughter Karen, son in law Graham and granddaughters Claire and Lexie for their computer expertise.

Finally to the sponsor for providing the financial backing – my wife's half of our joint bank account

Prologue

In the autumn of 2007, at the age of 69, I fell over on the tennis court in attempting to return serve. My upper body and racket arm moved to the right but my feet remained rooted to the spot. The ball had been struck by a retired surgeon and his partner, looking menacing at the net was, and still is, a GP.

I think they both knew at once what the problem was and advised me to see my doctor, who is also a tennis player. Eventually, in January 2008, I was diagnosed as having Parkinson's disease. Although Robert Porter, the GP on court at the time, had called round with a Christmas card in December, pointed his finger at me and told me face to face what I had suspected.

This meant the end of an undistinguished but varied and enjoyable sporting career, the details of which, according to my next-door neighbour Marjorie Harrison, an author and historian, ought to be preserved.

I have managed to complete the typing involved despite the fact that, although my hands do not shake, I do not have full control over my fingers. This has meant that the odd expletive has passed my lips; however I would counter this problem by looking out of the bedroom window and, on seeing Appleton Roebuck church, would return to my normal calm and serene temperament.

I invite you to find a comfortable chair with a glass of something you fancy by your side and enjoy.

John Waterhouse

The author aged 10 years

Any profit made on the publication of this book will be donated to the Parkinson's Disease Society

CHAPTER ONE

Rugby Union

I left Farsley Frances Street Primary School when I was 10 years old and went to Bradford Grammar School where the winter game was rugby union. My mother said that I started shooting up (in height – not what might be interpreted by that expression now) in my last year at school and when I went to work at Midland Bank.

Aged 10, I was small and in my view, not suited at all for rugby union, which came over to me as a game where brute force rather skill appeared to prevail. After being taught how to tackle and pass the ball, a school team was selected and it was no surprise when my name was not included; unfortunately this meant I played for the 'also rans' against the elite on a Thursday afternoon. I discovered that scrum- half or stand-off behind a beaten pack was not really the place to be and as soon as I found that I could opt out and have an afternoon of cross-country running followed by basketball and then 30 minutes in the swimming pool, I said cheerio to rugger.

When the inter- house competition came round, out of loyalty, I did not mind when my name was pencilled in at stand-off. Our pack of forwards usually won the battle up front and there were none of the nightmares I suffered before.

Two matches stand out in my memory. We conceded an early try and then went on to score about sixty points without any reply from our opponents. I was the goal kicker and, rather than kick the ball with my toe end, as was the vogue at the time, I copied the style initially used by Willie Horne who was the Great Britain rugby league stand- off; it was really like kicking a soccer ball and is now widely used in both codes of rugby. The House Master was intrigued; he clearly was a union stalwart and did not watch rugby league but encouraged me to continue. This was probably because I had popped the ball over the bar about a dozen times, and while most had been in front of the posts, one was a spectacular effort from the left wing which curled in late in flight

The second match was between our form and the rest of our year. The day before the game, one of our players did not arrive at school but a sick note did. Naturally, a reserve moved up 'from the bench'. However, the following afternoon, the illness had disappeared and our invalid turned up. Nobody at the time realised we had sixteen players and our defence coped very well with long kicks up field by our opponents as we had a full back on either side of the field. Roy Margerison scrambled over in the corner in the last minute and we won by a point After the game we realised what had happened and adhered to the maxim 'If in doubt do nowt'; someone blabbed and we were castigated by the Headmaster in morning assembly. That, some may say appropriately, was the last match in which I played.

When we were living in Menston I went to Otley to watch a county match – Huddersfield Town must have been playing away! I enjoyed the match which Yorkshire won with a late try, but the highlight of the afternoon was the warm pork pie at half time.

Together with millions of others I watched the World Cup Final when England beat Australia; I was not alone in realising that Jonny Wilkinson was going to drop a goal and my right foot was itching. This inspired me to watch other games on television – what an improvement since 'shamateurism' was replaced by open professionalism.

My wife prefers rugby league and if there is a clash of programmes, I take the easy way out; if only Leeds Carnegie could establish themselves in the top flight, I could be tempted to spend a Sunday afternoon at Headingley.

CHAPTER TWO

Cross Country Running

You may recall from the previous chapter that my interest in cross-country running was born out of a distinct lack of enthusiasm for rugby union. My running career also ended on leaving school.

I enjoyed the Thursday afternoon run and looked forward to the school races which were split into under 13, under 15 and senior. I was eleven when I first took part, competing with at least half of the field being a year older. With no experience of running a cross country race, I maintained a comfortable pace and then with about a mile to go and with plenty left in the tank, I accelerated, passing scores of other runners and to my surprise finished in fourth place. If only I had gone quicker from the start and had raised my pace earlier. The race was comfortably won by a boy called Rhodes.

The next year I fancied my chances as Rhodes and the others who finished in front of me had to move up to the under 15 race. This time I decided to lead from the start; the tactic worked and I romped in first to earn a free bottle of lemonade at the unofficial tuck shop which was run by a guy called George. At first he would not pay out, hinting that I was too small but did so on confirmation from two of my friends.

In 1952 I was too old for the under 13 race and met up again with the dreaded Rhodes; he was too good for me but I finished in second place. For the next year's race the course was altered; we started with a long uphill pull from the Norman Arch to the top end of Manningham Park (Lister Park) round some roads in Heaton and then back down to the far end of the lake.

Winning the Bradford Grammar School
Junior Cross Country Race 1951

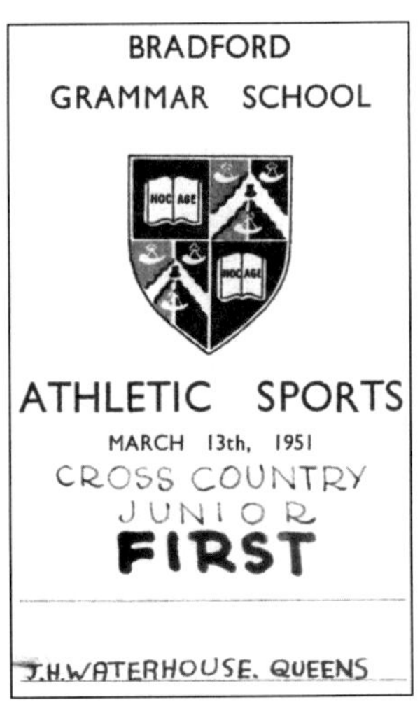
BRADFORD
GRAMMAR SCHOOL

ATHLETIC SPORTS
MARCH 13th, 1951
CROSS COUNTRY
JUNIOR
FIRST

J.H.WATERHOUSE. QUEENS

My efforts to lead from the front were thwarted by Philip Bailey, or Bailey JP as he was known formally. I trailed him along Toller Lane, down the park and then, as Baldrick of Blackadder fame would have done, I devised a cunning plan. The path round the side of the lake had several bends and Philip was running in the middle. When he could not see me I accelerated and overtook him on the near side – no point in risking falling into the lake.He had led for most of the race but not where it mattered and I won by two yards. George, the tuck shop man, paid out with no questions asked.

In 1954, my last race, I was in the senior group with some of the other runners up to three years older than me. This was too much of a handicap and coupled with the effects of growing I only managed 13th place.

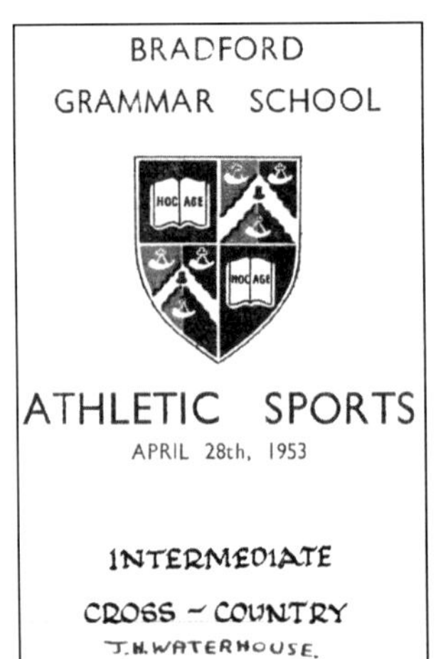
BRADFORD
GRAMMAR SCHOOL

ATHLETIC SPORTS
APRIL 28th, 1953

INTERMEDIATE
CROSS – COUNTRY
J.H. WATERHOUSE.
FIRST

Occasionally we had races against other schools and the master in charge of cross-country running, Mr Atkinson, entered a team in the Halifax and District Championships. The course was on the hills around Halifax and I recall it was bitterly cold. Most of the other competitors, from established clubs, were older than me and I thought 25th out of 80 entrants was not too bad. My day was made when I was told that our team had finished 3rd in the team event and, as the last qualifier, I was entitled to a medal.

After leaving school I went to some training sessions at Bramley and District Harriers but the lure of football and cricket was too strong.

CHAPTER THREE

Playing Football

My first experiences of playing football were in the playground at Farsley Frances Street Primary School and it was then that I learned how important sport can be. One Monday morning a new boy appeared in our class and we were a bit surprised that he did not seem to know his name. It turned out that his mother who had a baker's shop had re-married, and Tommy was not sure whether he was Tommy Bradley or Tommy Sparling. He settled for the former. He was a somewhat timid boy, not happy in his new surroundings and his mother asked mine if I would take him under my wing. Soon he grew in confidence as his football skills improved. One afternoon his mother was going over to the bake house, which was across the street from the shop, when she heard a great commotion and saw Tommy being chaired by two of the larger boys with several others thronging round. What had happened? Tommy had scored the winning goal in a vital playground match and was being hailed as a hero. He stayed in the village for many years taking over the shop when his parents retired – something he would not have thought possible after his first two days at school.

Unfortunately, it was shortly after I left to go to Bradford Grammar School that a school team was formed and so my first taste of participating in an organised team was to come eight years later.

A group of my friends had been kicking a ball about in Hainsworth Park on Sunday afternoons for some time when we were joined by Dennis Faulkner, Bill Wilkinson and others who were trying to form a team based at Reuben Gaunt's mill but found they were short of a few players.

No prizes for guessing what happened next and on a sunny day in September 1956, Reubens Gaunt's AFC ran out on to the field at East End Park, Leeds in our blue shirts to face Hathorn Davey Sports in Division H.(Yes H is the eighth letter in the alphabet). The Sports and Social Club at the mill has been only too pleased to lash out some money on a worthwhile project and didn't we look smart!.

At half time, we were leading one-nil and I am delighted to say I scored the club's first goal with a rasping right foot drive following a mix-up in our opponents' defence. However at the interval we realised what a shambles we were off the field; our visitors had water, oranges and a first-aid kit. We had nothing but enthusiasm.

Early in the second half Hathorn Davey equalised and put us under pressure; it was then we had a piece of luck. A long desperate clearance from our huge centre half, Arthur Coggins, landed over the heads of their defence and I was able to race through unopposed to slide the ball into the left hand corner of the net and restore our lead.

I dropped back into defence to help to stem the tide of incessant attacks and with not long to go, Arthur had the ball at his feet in the centre circle; his first touch and indeed his second, third and fourth touches were not his strength and I was about to shout ' Get rid Arthur' when he rampaged forward, scattering defenders in his wake and scored a superb goal. My strangled cry of 'Get rid' was quickly changed to 'Good goal'. The referee blew his whistle and we had won an epic encounter 3-1.The following week we were brought down to earth losing 5-2 at home to a team called All Saints whose name did not reflect the way they played the game but at least we now had a first-aid box – and oranges at half time.

I knew at the start of the 1956/1957 season that I would not play many matches as I was about to be called up to do National Service and when I travelled down to Portsmouth to join the Royal Army Ordnance Corps on the first of November, Reubens Gaunt's were in the top half of the table and I had scored 16 goals in 8 matches. We did have a lot of high scoring games as big Arthur, who was supposed to be the pivot of our defence was prone to wander out of position..

The first five weeks of basic training were hectic but I did not mind the physical exercise and, in the sixth and final week when our group had clearly done quite well, the Sergeant Major organised a football match between our Hut, number 29, and Hut 30. This was not a fixture for Football Focus but it was the hardest match in which I have ever played, particularly as there were not enough boots in the stores and so we all wore the standard army issue plimsolls, somewhat flimsy footwear far removed from the trainers which are in vogue these days. The result was 2-2 leaving all the players with a healthy respect for each other.

After completing my training to be a clerk, I was posted to the permanent staff of the trade training battalion at Blackdown, Aldershot. Possibly this had something to do with the fact that the Chief Clerk of Storeman Company was Barrie (Sorry, Corporal) Carter who lived in Summerville Road, Farsley. At first this was OK, but after a while became boring and the highlight of the week was the football match each Wednesday afternoon. The battalion team was made up by the professional players and so Barrie and I played for the company team.

The battalion side was not having much success and it was no surprise when they were knocked out of a cup competition in the first round. This meant the Charlie Rackstraw who worked in Barrie's office but who also played inside forward for Chesterfield in Division 3 North in the Football League was available for selection. Charlie was told he would not get in the company side at inside- forward despite his obvious ability as Corporal Carter played inside-left and I played inside- right and Corporal Carter and I picked the team – he played a blinder at centre-half!!

Soon after the football season ended, I decided that the job I was doing was too boring and it was arranged that I would have the pick of the postings from the next batch of trainees who completed their course. Choice? It was Bicester or Bicester – a large RAOC depot near Oxford which supplied the requirements of the British Army of the Rhine which was still stationed in Germany. There was no organised football and in October 1958 I completed my two year stint and returned home to Farsley.

During the previous summer I had met Alan Pannett who played cricket at Pudsey Britannia and he invited me to join him at Bramley Wanderers AFC if I needed a club for the next football season. Reuben Gaunts had been a one-season wonder and so I decided to play at Bramley in Division A – a bit of a step up from Division H!

The season was two months old when I made my debut on the home pitch which sloped from touchline to touchline. As usual Wanderers were struggling near the foot of the table and we lost 5-1 but I did manage to notch the goal. The next match was also at home with the score line and the goal scorer the same.

I had not been long at the club when the draw was made for the Leeds and District Senior Cup; there was great excitement in the camp when we drew local rivals Swinnow Athletic. Some of the Swinnow players had also played at Bramley and their side included Mick Tobin who played cricket at

Pudsey Britannia. There was also a connection between Bramley Wanderers and the Brit as Eric Vevers and Billy Woolford had played for both clubs and now there was Alan Pannett and myself. Swinnow were doing well in a lower division and there was the prospect of a giant – killing on their pitch against opponents from the top division. The prospect became a reality but I did manage to get a couple a good tackles in on the Swinnow playmaker, Mick Tobin.

In another cup competition we were drawn away to Market District Boys Club whose pitch was by the side of the A64 near the Shaftesbury cinema. The playing area was rather narrow and this made throw-ins and corners more dangerous to defend. We got a corner on the left; this was to be taken by a young man whose name escapes me but who used to arrive for matches wearing his football shirt – black and white stripes as per Newcastle United – with a red tie and and a jacket.He thought this was the height of sartorial elegance. I was playing at right half and was lurking on the edge of the penalty area to snap up any mishit clearance. 'Tie man' fired the ball in with great pace and I ran in to the far post, anticipating the ball to clear all the other players. As I was getting ready for a header, the ball took a deflection and struck me a painful blow on the knee making me fall to the ground writhing in agony. I thought the sympathy shown by my teammates was over the top until it dawned on me that I had scored. The ball had found the top corner giving the goalkeeper no chance. A goal to remember but one I never saw. If you happen to be on a bus going towards Leeds and as you pass under the huge footbridge with football pitches on your left you see an elderly man with grey hair and glasses begin to smile, please do not send for the men in white coats, it will be me having nostalgic moment.

By the time March came round we were still near the foot of the table and I had been switched permanently to wing-half. The turning point in our season was the local derby against Upper Armley Old Boys who were challenging for the title. Their key man was their inside left called Longbottom through whom most of their attacking moves were channelled; not so that day as he limped off after an hour having been on the receiving end of a series of heavy tackles from the Bramley right half.

His absence left me free to venture up field and after a mazy run which took me past four of their players I created an opening for a colleague who shot wide. The report in the Pudsey and Stanningley News said that I was reluctant to shoot – the truth was I was too tired. We scrambled a goal late on and then held out for a lucky 1-0 win and narrowly avoided relegation in the last match of the season.

The pitch at Bramley was on land mainly consisting of clay and it became extremely heavy after a spell of wet weather. This led to postponements and fixtures being re-arranged in evenings towards the end of the season. For most of the team this meant travelling straight from work with nothing to eat. This is where Dave, who collected our insurance money and did other sundry jobs, came into his own. His day job was driving a van for a bakery and he could be guaranteed to have some pies and pasties which, he said, would only be thrown away the next day. We saved him the trouble. After the match a couple of Dave's pies and a pint or two of Tetley's was a treat to look forward to.

One of the benefits of playing at Bramley Wanderers was the provision of a physiotherapy service. Peter Cooper, our club secretary was, in his day job, the Company Secretary at Jabez Woolley Brickworks where the night-watchman was Arthur Crampton, a former masseur at Leeds Rugby League club. Arthur's claim to fame, as he would tell people ad nauseum, was that he used to rub down Arthur Clues, the big Australian forward who was a legend in the city of Leeds for many years.

I had severe bruising on my right leg after George Atack left his foot in and I went to see Arthur Crampton one evening. In between doing his rounds he had me lying on the Board Room table while he applied an evil smelling embrocation suitably embellished by the ash which periodically fell from Arthur's cigarette, and then put me under the lamp which did not have any control over the amount of heat – it was either on at full or off altogether. I kept complaining but all Arthur would say was ' Doing it good, lad'

In the morning I had a huge blister on my leg and so I missed two matches instead of one. These were to be the only matches where I was unfit to play in any sport whether it was football, cricket or tennis.

I declared myself fit for the local derby at Horsforth Wanderers. The pitch at Horsforth had a pronounced slope which went diagonally from corner to corner and in the first minute, the ball skidded off the greasy turf, hit me on the shin pad and burst the blister. After five minutes of agony, the pain gradually wore off and a 2-1 victory made the sacrifice worthwhile. Now, 51 years later, I still have an indentation on my leg.

I generally played well whenever we met Beeston St Anthony's (The Tonies). Towards the end of a season, on a bumpy pitch, I received the ball about 25 yards from goal and was quickly being closed down. I decided to shoot and side footed the ball on the rise with the result that it ballooned high into the air spinning like a top in the direction of the goal. At the time Scottish goalkeepers were having a bad time at international level and the Beeston keeper was Scottish(I assumed that because his colleagues kept calling him Jock.) Clearly he did not wish to buck the trend for keepers from the other side of Hadrian's Wall and let the viciously spinning ball slip from his grasp. It then hit his head and rolled into the net. What a goal. The report in the local newspaper read something on the lines of Waterhouse saw the Beeston goalkeeper off his line and from 25 yards unleashed an unstoppable shot into the top corner – the spin on the ball would have done credit to Jim Laker. Who am I to disagree!!

The glut of fixtures also affected the second team and one week they were scheduled to play on Monday, Wednesday and Friday in order to complete their matches before the end of the season. It was decided to play the first team on the Wednesday against Forgrove Sports who, unknown to our committee, needed only one point to clinch the top spot in Division 1F.As we were in Division 1A it was the equivalent of a side near the bottom of the Premier League playing a team in Conference North and the result reflected the gulf in class. We won 6-1 and the league officials who had come to present the cup, had to take it back. Fortunately Forgrove had another game to play and won their Division.

Just after Christmas someone at Barclays Bank in Bradford was looking around the vault and discovered the Algernon Denham Trophy. Enquiries around the other banks failed to provide any details as to who the gentleman was or what it was played for. It was decided therefore, to organise a football competition towards the end of the season. Four teams entered and our team, Midland Bank were drawn against Barclays with Lloyds to play Yorkshire Penny. We scraped through our match but it looked as if we would not be able to get enough players for the final due to injuries, wives' worries about injuries, holidays and other sundry excuses. However we were not alone as Yorkshire Penny, our cup final opponents were also struggling.

As luck would have it Bramley Wanderers played Meanwood Trinity on the Saturday before the final and three of their players were joking about guesting for a bank team in a match in Bradford the following Wednesday. I took note of this and thoughts of geese and ganders came to mind. Bearing in mind the old maxim that if you cheat you have got to win, I enrolled five Bramley players to strengthen the Midland team.

I was not too concerned about this deception as I had decided that banking was not for me and would soon be seeking pastures new We won the match and took the cup back to our branch the following day receiving congratulations all round. However we were rumbled by someone from Yorkshire Penny who realised that we had, as it were, out-trumped them and spilled the beans. The trophy went back into the vault at Barclays and I got a rollicking from the branch manager.

Possibly someone at Barclays had an inkling that I had been involved in an incident a few months before. Five minutes before closing the bank one Friday

I was on the main counter when I sensed trouble. Anyone who has served behind a bar or counter can recognise a dodgy character. A man approached me and said 'Can you cash this please' proffering a Bradford Corporation bus ticket with a value of 4pence (old money). Fortunately I was quick enough to say, ' Sorry, wrong bank, you want Barclays just down the street, you can't miss it.'

Apparently, Barclays could not get rid of him and had to call the police with the man trying to explain that another bank had said it would be all right. On the Monday morning our manager came to the counter to see all the cashiers and said he had had a message from his counterpart at Barclays – did we know anything about it? To a man we answered 'No'. 'Thought not' he replied.' When I eventually left the bank, the manager, with a smile on his face, said 'hard luck at being caught out with the football match; but you were involved with the bus ticket weren't you?'

The next season did not start well for us but we hoped to progress in the Cup when we were drawn against a team in a lower division. I had a poor game at wing half as I was not getting the ball from our defence and seemed to have two opponents to tackle when they attacked. We lost 3-1 and I was asked if I wished to plug a gap in the second team at centre half. This was a polite way of dropping me and I could not disagree.

The first team again just avoided relegation while the second team with their defence now stiffened almost won promotion. As a reward for accepting the demotion and because I was known to all the players I received most votes and won the Player of the Year Award.

During the summer some of the first team players including Alan, either moved away or retired and although I regained my first team spot, I was not enjoying my game. I decided after a few games to join the nearest club in the league, Farnley, with the aim of being what is now termed a 'squad player' Farnley were always near the top of the league and did well in cup competitions.

Each Thursday there was a training session organised at Cow Close Secondary School after which everyone adjourned to Farnley Working Men's Club ostensibly to find out what the teams were but also to have a game of dominoes and the odd drink. I received a signing on fee – a pint of Tetley's mild and a bag of crisps – cheese and onion.

I was surprised when I was selected to play centre-half in what I think was a West Riding cup tie against Rolls Royce of Barnoldswick – possibly it was because there was little choice for the team selectors and that I had had a good game against Farnley about 3 weeks before. The match was played at Thwaite Gate Hunslet as the Farnley pitch was not enclosed. We won comfortably and

I found their centre- forward no problem – he was not very tall and had no pace. I also had good support from my new team mates.

My shortcomings were exposed in the next match against East Leeds WMC as their forwards created chance after chance down the middle. Barry Haxby, who later went on to play at a higher level, switched from left back and his more robust style and strength stemmed the tide.

A former Farnley player, Gerry Rogers returned to the club to play centre half but I was given another opportunity – this time at right half which was really my best position. I thought I had a reasonable game but found myself in the second team where, of course, I thought I would be anyway.

In September 1963, a football match was arranged between Farsley Celtic and Farsley Cricket Club. It was well advertised locally and on a fine Sunday afternoon, with no other attractions, a large crowd assembled. Our stars were Brian Hird and his younger brother Malcolm who were both on Celtic's books at the time. Celtic fielded largely a reserve team but took the game seriously. They led 1-0 at half time and scored again early in the second half. Malcolm reduced the arrears and for the next ten minutes Celtic had to step up a gear. Shortly after they scored their third goal, the ref blew for time. I thought the second half was long and the referee explained that after 45 minutes everyone was enjoying themselves, including the crowd, and so he only stopped the game when Celtic scored in the 57th minute. Apparently it was one of the larger crowds of the season at Throstle Nest.

The next season went well for both teams and apart from two matches when I was selected at centre forward in the first team due to the suspension of the regular player, I consolidated my place in the second team.

However I was selected for the final match with the first team and thought it odd when the team sheet didn't show what position any of us were playing. As there was nothing at stake it had been decided that the more senior players would allocate the positions on arrival at our opponents' ground, Slazengers Sports in Wakefield. The goalkeeper fancied his chances at centre forward while our tricky left winger wanted to play in goal. Harry Lister, a cultured wing half, who went on to play for Halifax Town and Boston United moved to centre half while Norman Alderson, our tough tackling full back, went up to play inside- forward as did our other full back. I slotted in a left -back which meant that in a career which began at Reuben Gaunts and progressed via National Service, Bramley Wanderers and Farnley, I had been selected to start in every outfield position. Was it a case of versatility or overall mediocrity?

Slazengers did not know what hit them; Norman, tackling like the full-back he was, ensured they did not play through midfield as was their normal style while Harry gobbled up the long balls as he later said 'Just like supping tea' We won 6-0 but what a pity our new centre forward could not find the net.

1964 Leeds & District Cup Final – Farnley in plain shirts
Harry Lister (6), Gerry Rogers (5) and Barry Haxby (3)

I thought my season had ended with the second team having completed their fixtures but the first team had one game left, The Leeds and District FA Cup Final at Elland Road. During the first half Eric Alderson was injured, but in those days, there was no rule on substitutes and he had to soldier on. I was the logical replacement if the match was drawn and with the score at 0-0 and time running out, my hopes were high. Unfortunately, we conceded a goal direct from a corner in the last minute. This was a double whammy; we had lost and I was not going to play at the home of Leeds United.

In my third season, the second team won their division in the league and reached the final of the league cup competition, The Major Knight Trophy. We were all set to do the double but when I arrived at the LICS ground I sensed that something was wrong. Horace Coulson, the power behind the throne on the committee had been killed in a motor accident the previous day. Nowadays the match would have been postponed but not then; at least six of the team only learned about Horace as I had. Our hearts were not in it and we went down to a late disputed penalty rammed home by Henry Idle, a former colleague at Bramley, who had come out of retirement to play for J & S Sports (Jowett and Sowry, the Leeds printing company). A long clearance from Henry had bounced up from the greasy turf and hit our left back on the arm, right in the corner of the penalty area, with no opponent within 20 yards. Even the J & S Sports players thought the ref had given a corner.

We stayed for a while after the game but the atmosphere was subdued and the winners did not deem it fit to celebrate either. In the bus queue later I had words with the referee who looked somewhat shamefaced but one of the linesmen said ' You have a go if you think you can do better'.

It was a sad ending to what was an enjoyable spell at Farnley; Sandra and I were married in December and I had already decided it was too far to travel from Menston to Farnley by bus to start another season. I now had the summer to mull over what to do next season.

At this point I thought my playing days were over. They certainly were as regards competitive football but when I joined the Wharfedale Referees Association the opportunity arose to play for their own team in friendly matches. We entered a 5 a side competition to be played at Fullerton Park which was the football pitch at the rear of the West Stand at Elland Road. As one of the smaller associations in the West Riding Area we did not fancy our chances but nevertheless, found ourselves in the quarter-final with the match official being from the Football League list. He clearly did not want to be there and made his feelings known which irked both us and our opponents.

To referee a match in which the players want to cause problems is difficult, but where those players are referees themselves it is impossible. After a while things settled down when, a truce was called. One of the rules of the competition was that if the scores were level at full time, the numbers of corners would count. Our match was going to be close and so, when the ball went out for a goal kick, I picked it up and went to take a corner. The ref was not sure whether it was a goal kick or a corner but was duped by my confident action and so we were ahead albeit one corner to nil.

Inevitably with all the pressure on our defence, we conceded a goal and so with one minute to go we were losing 1 -0 but of course would win the tie if we could equalise. I managed to get into the penalty area and fell with exhaustion against a defender; the whistle went – penalty!!

The kick was successful and we were in the semi final where our luck ran out, and we were soundly beaten. This meant we could enjoy a couple of pints watching the second semi-final and then the final and could reflect on an enjoyable day.

In January 1970 Sandra and I moved to a house on a new development (a posh word for estate) which almost doubled the population of Appleton Roebuck by the time it was completed.Unfortunately a 'them and us' situation was apparent and so in order to bring the two halves of the village together, a football match was arranged. The intention was to play in the morning and finish off in the local. Our team of newcomers had a reasonable side. One of our players, Norman Lowe could claim that his sister-in-law was married to Paul Reaney the Leeds United and England right back. The actual match was one-sided and we ran out comfortable winners much to the disgust of the 'old villagers' who sloped off to the Roebuck Inn while we took liquid refreshment at the Shoulder of Mutton. Clearly the idea of promoting unity failed miserably.

In the early seventies, John Walker, his wife and her parents ran the Happy Wanderer, a roadhouse and pub on the A64 catering mainly for coach parties returning from the east coast on their way back to the West Riding. When our local pub in Appleton Roebuck was closed for renovation, I with one or two others took it in turns to drive up to the Happy Wanderer. John was a keen Liverpool fan and formed a football team from his regular clientele. Somehow I was dragged in and found myself playing at right back against a Bishopthorpe United team of youngsters and old hands. Their left winger was a young lad but he did appear to be a tad overweight. He got the ball and I ambled towards him. There was no way that both the ball and the man were going to get past me together. It was going to be one or the other.

Sure enough, the youth pushed the ball down the line but I managed to turn and get to the ball before him despite being twice his age; foul tactics were not required. At half time we were 6-nil up. Bishopthorpe made some changes in their team as had been previously agreed and my immediate opponent was consigned to the bench. The final score of 6-4 reflected a change of fortunes for us in the second half but we held on to qualify for a few free pints.

The curtain fell on my career but on a winning note.

CHAPTER 4

Refereeing Football

Following the traumatic events at the LICS ground, I forgot about football for a while and concentrated on playing cricket; however I met Bob Armstrong who had recently moved into Menston from the Manchester area. Bob was an experienced referee and had recently applied to the Football League for inclusion on to their panel of officials. A couple of weeks later I saw him in the paper shop and the broad smile on his face said it all. He was to referee reserve games for the top division clubs interspersed with running the line in the lower divisions of the league.

That was the clincher and I enrolled on the referee training course organised by the Wharfedale Football Association. The instructor was Ken Rhodes and there were ten of us budding whistlers.

I was studying for the examinations of the Institute of Chartered Secretaries part of which involved Law and coupled with my playing experience passed the test at the end of the course and became a referee Class 3.

At the time, referees offered their services to whichever league they fancied and, using the Wisdom of Solomon, I decided to officiate in Leeds for the first two weeks in the month with the remaining weeks in the local Wharfedale League. I felt this was the right thing to do as I had played all my football in Leeds but done my training in Wharfedale.

The season was under way and refereeing appointments already made for the opening matches, when, one Friday evening, I got a call telling me that I was required to take charge of Shipley Town v Ives Sports as Arthur Scroggins, who had been appointed, was ill. Arthur was a very experienced

Wharfedale Referees Association Annual Dinner 1966
John and Sandra – first and second from the left

referee and I was surprised that I was to take his place. Ives Sports were the previous season's champions and current league leaders while Shipley Town were the local equivalent of Millwall.

In a tense game, Ives Sports won 3-2 thanks to two penalties and the fact that Shipley had a man sent off. The player I dismissed remained on the touch line still wearing his shirt. There were no linesmen appointed which meant I gave the offside decisions and he was a distraction. I told him to put on a tracksuit top and stand with the trainer near the half way line. At this point he was clearly not pleased and called me various names, including a little Hitler preceded by words which I will not repeat. I objected to this but said nothing at the time – I did not look remotely like Hitler and did not have a moustache.

After that baptism of fire, the next few matches were uneventful by comparison in both Leeds and Wharfedale. My performances must have been satisfactory as I was appointed to referee a cup semi-final in Leeds and had my first experience of operating with linesmen. This came in useful as I was asked to run the line in a local semi in Wharfedale.

Towards the end of each season Otley football club ran a workshops competition where the competing teams came from local places of employment, pubs and clubs. The main rule was that only five members of the team could be regular players with the remainder being veterans or young lads. Bob Armstrong advised me to give it a miss, but I felt out of loyalty to the local football community to offer my services.

I had covered a couple of matches but then the weather deteriorated and there were several postponements. In a few days the pitch was declared fit and one Tuesday evening I got on the bus to Otley to take charge of Shires

Sanitary Ware against the New Inn, a local derby. Each match was scheduled to last 30 minutes with extra time to be played of 5 minutes each way with two further such periods if necessary.

The scores were level at 4-4 when we entered the final 5 minutes of extra time. The gloom had gathered several minutes previously and the lights of the clubhouse shone out like beacons. With seconds to go a player from Shires smashed the ball into the net from close range. There were some muffled appeals for offside but I had seen nothing wrong – in fact I had not seen much at all. I blew for full time and returned to the referee's changing room which in former life must have been a broom cupboard. The Otley club treasurer came in with my fee and expenses amounting to nine shillings and with the usual cup of tea there was a chocolate biscuit. He said it was a reward for using my discretion because of the previous postponements in allowing that offside goal.

There was a further reward in that I was appointed to referee one of the semi-finals. In this competition the stronger teams progress but sometimes one of the less fancied teams, with a bit of luck, and an easy draw did quite well. I found that my match involved one of the surprise teams against the favourites. Presumably the organisers thought the game would be one-sided and that a rookie referee could cope especially as I had two experienced linesmen.

Kick-off was 2.30pm on a Sunday afternoon and, as most of the drinking establishments in Otley at the time closed at 2pm, a large boisterous crowd turned up no doubt attracted more by the fact that the bar remained open, rather than a football match. Sandra had come to add moral support and stood near the half way line.The linesmen on her side of the pitch was Dave Brotherton, a well known Otley character.

After 20 minutes with the favourites already three goals ahead, I was aware of some barracking from a large rotund gentleman who was standing not far from Sandra. In due course when it was clear that his inane comments were not having effect, he said to Dave ‘ Who is yon b....r, nivver seen him afore, where've you dragged him up from then?' Dave had a wicked sense of humour and instead of sticking up for me, openly encouraged his new found friend. At half time I got my slice of orange and went over for a word with Sandra when, of course, it was obvious who she was. Sandra gave him one of her stares that kill at ten paces and he disappeared back into the bar.

The second half was one way traffic and with ten minutes to go, the heavens opened with torrential rain sweeping down from the Chevin. All the spectators raced for shelter in the clubhouse leaving the players and officials rapidly getting soaked. With the score at 7-0, the captain of the losing side said they had had enough and would not mind if the match ended there and then. The other captain concurred and so I blew my whistle. Another case of referee's discretion!

The Appointments Secretary for the various leagues in Leeds was a gentleman by the name of Robin (Jock) Robin who had been the secretary of Leysholme Amateurs, a team located on the western side of Leeds and rivals of both Bramley Wanderers and Farnley; Jock knew me and maybe that was why I got the appointment for that semi-final in my first season. I officiated in a few good matches, particularly when the originally appointed referee became unavailable as Jock knew I would change my plans at short notice.

I received a call from him one Friday evening asking me to switch from my league fixture and to take a cup replay. I hadn't given much thought to the change, although usually the referee who does the original match is in charge for the replay. Jock gave me the directions as I had not been to this particular ground before, with the instructions that, if necessary, there would be extra time. No penalty shoot-outs or silver or golden goals in those days.

I set off in plenty of time and arrived quite early, in fact, just as the groundsman was putting up the goal nets. After an inspection of the ground markings, I ventured over to look at the goal nets at which point I was asked if I was the referee.' Hmm' came the reply 'I hope tha's better than daft b.... r we had last week' 'Oh', I enquired 'what happened then?' Apparently my colleague had lost control and had abandoned the match with 10 minutes to go with the majority of the players fighting in the centre -circle. Thank you Jock Robin!! I got a couple of good decisions in early on in the game which won the players confidence and before half time I was able to play the advantage rule. The home side won 5-4 in what turned out to be a cracking match. Both captains thanked me and I went home feeling ten feet tall.

In 1967 the 4- step rule was introduced at all levels of the game and, needless to say, the grass roots officials were the last to get any instructions. Bob Armstrong was running the line in a pre-season friendly at Huddersfield. The referee was the experienced official from Bolton by the name of A Hamer who told us he had just come back from holiday and asked what this 4-step rule was all about. Bob explained as well as he could on limited information and somehow the game went smoothly. For my first match, I decided that Bob's interpretation was correct and after the captains had tossed up, called both 'keepers to the middle. I told them about the new rule and said I would use my discretion for the first 10 minutes. I thought I had a good game, probably because I had got off on the right foot – ever the diplomat! Two top marks that day surely.

Usually on the Saturday before Christmas the programme was blank but sometimes teams with a fixture backlog took the opportunity to arrange a match. Smiths Sports of Rodley did just this and I was asked to referee their game against the league leaders.

Smiths only had ten men and lost 9-0 although in their team they had the best individual player. On the way back to the changing rooms this young man was openly criticising me with a comment something like 'What chance have you with a blankety blank like that in charge ?.'

I pretended not to hear and continued on my way; he then came face to face with me and, as I said in my subsequent report, used foul and abusive language. At this point I took his name and told him I was sending him off. He laughed, thinking he could say what he liked after the final whistle, and said he would appeal if I dared to report him. I did and he did but he failed to attend the hearing and was heavily fined. What pity his temperament did not match his ability. I wonder if he enjoyed Christmas.

One of the problems in operating without official linesmen occurs when a team deliberately tries to get the opposing forwards offside. Burley Liberal Club, a side of experienced players, some of whom had lost that extra yard of pace, were taking on Pudsey Juniors, several of whose players had had, or were still having, trials with Football League clubs. They were a young fit team with plenty of youthful enthusiasm and fitness. Burley caught the Pudsey forwards offside repeatedly and the youngsters had no answer to a tactic which was completely new to them. In the second half their coach positioned himself on the touchline in the Burley half no doubt to check whether my decisions were correct. At the end of the game, which Burley won 4-1, he congratulated me on my performance; no doubt his coaching during the week would include how to beat the offside trap.

Another team to use the offside tactic played in the Yorkshire Old Boys League. They were successful in coping with their superior opponents in a terrible boring game until five minutes from time. Three defenders raised their hands once again to appeal for offside only to discover to their horror that the left back has stayed in the penalty area to re-tie his boot lace thereby playing the attacker onside. I waited until I had turned my back before I had a wry smile and signalled the only goal of the game.

Not too many referees will have received a caution from their local Football Association but I have that dubious honour. I was at Myrtle Park, Bingley for a cup match. Sandra thought it would be a good idea to come along with Karen and Jane (daughters). On arrival I found that the hut which doubles up as a store for goal nets and corner flags and also as the changing rooms had been vandalised. The Bingley players were doing their best to tidy up and at the same time prepare for the match. The two players in charge of pitch markings clearly had not done the job before. One started with the half way line from the far side and his mate from the side nearest the hut. It was a case of never the twain shall meet and some hurried realignment of sawdust had to take place.

The goal nets had been slashed by the vandals and were not really fit for purpose but were better than nothing. The ball had a split in the case but as it was all the club had and we had to make the best of it. Meanwhile Sandra and the girls had departed for the shops and the match kicked off some 45 minutes late.

In the first half the visitors' centre forward had a shot at goal tipped over the bar by the Bingley goalkeeper but to everyone's horror the ball continued on its way into the nearby river Aire. As this was the only ball it had to be retrieved. Fortunately one of the visiting players was a good swimmer and after executing an excellent racing dive swam towards the ball which was tantalisingly being carried from him by the current. Eventually he caught up with it and the game could continue. The Bingley players wanted to re-start immediately but I insisted on waiting for our swimming hero to dry himself and put on his shirt and boots. By the time I blew for half time, the shopping party had returned and came on to the pitch thinking the match was over. Sorry, girls another 45 minutes yet.

The second half was not as eventful as the first apart from the visitors scoring three goals to win the match. The reason for the caution? On completing my match report I had described the goal nets as four holes tied together. The gentlemen of the Wharfedale FA did not share my sense of humour.

At the start of the 1968/69 season, I applied for promotion which this time involved being watched with my performance being assessed by three people on separate occasions. Attracted by the lure of a huge salary, I had accepted a position from Standard Telephones and Cables at Harlow in Essex with a starting date in January and so I asked the Wharfedale FA if I could have all my assessments completed by the end of December. Despite my indiscretion at Bingley, they agreed and, although I was not supposed to know which matches were involved, I was able to work out the first two occasions and so there remained the third.

I was appointed to a game at Ilkley in mid December and I knew that the Secretary of the Ilkley club was an assessor. On looking at the team sheets I noticed the name of the Ilkley number 11 was the same as the Secretary, presumably his son. The game was not particularly memorable although I recall that Ilkley won comfortably. On my way out of the changing rooms, I was asked by the home team captain if I would choose a man of the match. Guess who? Yes the number 11! My promotion was later approved.

One Good Friday I went with Bob Armstrong to Hartlepool when the visitors were Luton Town; Bob was one of the linesmen. We had set off early and even though the traffic was quite heavy, we arrived just on the scheduled time i.e. one hour before kick-off. The referee joined us 15 minutes later but still no sign of the other linesman who eventually turned up only a couple of minutes before the referee was going to ask me to get my gear out of Bob's car. In a way, I was relieved although the officials had no problems with 'Pool winning 5-1.

The match at Ilkley turned out to be my last of the season. I was travelling from Harlow each weekend arriving home at 9pm on Friday evening and setting off back at 5pm on a Sunday afternoon. I did not feel like refereeing and I don't think Sandra would have been too pleased either. After a few weeks, Sandra and the girls moved down to Harlow where we had a rented house. However, the job did not work out and with Karen due to start school I decided to move back to Yorkshire.

I took up a position with Hargreaves Fertilisers in York and after living in the city centre for a few months, moved to Appleton Roebuck. I picked up the refereeing and found there were several differences from what I had been used to. The distances were much greater, a complete change from Wharfedale, I did not know any of the players and there was no Jock Robin to hand out the favours.

Easter 1970 highlighted these problems. On the Saturday Copmanthorpe AFC entertained a Swiss club. I refereed the first match between the two reserve sides and later in the afternoon ran the line when the first teams played. Sunday saw me at Pickering contending with the holiday traffic going to the east coast and then on Monday morning I had an appointment at Riccall. Fortunately I could get to Leeds Road, Huddersfield to watch Town draw 2-2 with Hull City.

Towards the end of the season, my refereeing appointment was at Coxwold and, as it was a bright sunny morning, we decided to take Karen(4 and a bit years old) and Jane(a year younger) on the basis that they would have more space to run around than in the yard behind the flat we were renting. The football field was a mile or so from the village but the girls were quite happy.

Just as I was about to walk on to the field, the proverbial man arrived, not with his dog, but riding a bicycle. What was odd was that he only had one leg, on which he wore a wellington boot. In a loud piping voice that children have at what turn out to be embarrassing moments, Jane said 'Mummy that man only has one leg – how does he ride his bike?' I abdicated all responsibility and left it for Sandra to sort out. However, before she could think what to say, Jane by this time in full flow said 'What does he do with his other wellington boot?'

Fortunately the man was deaf and was oblivious to the smirks and titters emanating from the players who clearly had sympathy with Sandra and me. This created a good atmosphere and unwittingly Jane paved the way for me to have a good game. Somehow I could not see this happening to a referee at a Premier League match.

This hectic programme coupled with the fact that a large full back from Dringhouses had suggested a visit to the opticians might prove to be beneficial and the return of Huddersfield to the first division prompted my decision to hang up my whistle.

I enjoyed refereeing, going to different places each week and had the satisfaction that I had put something back into the game. The gentleman from Dringhouses was correct in his diagnosis as a visit to the optician saw me wearing glasses from then on.

CHAPTER 5

Billiards and Snooker

I first picked up a cue at the Men's Institute at Farsley Church having been to watch my father play matches in the Pudsey and District Sunday Schools Billiards League. Due to other distractions such as school, home work and travelling to and from school in Bradford I had not taken any interest in the game unlike some of my friends who had made the effort and were then reasonably competent players. When one of the regular second team players was ill, I was given a chance and did not let the side down even though I lost my match 64-100. The format of a match was that the five members of the team each played one game with an opponent, with the winner being the first to score 100 points (125 points in the first team).

As a change in mid- season there was a snooker tournament but I got the impression this was a bit of light relief rather than a serious competition. I was once allowed to play for the fourth team – there were only three members in each team – but needless to say I lost my frame. In the early 1950's there was no television to promote snooker; the situation changed when Pot Black which was popular when it was introduced to the small screen.

The Yorkshire Evening Post, the local Leeds newspaper, organised a billiards handicap tournament and Alan Smith of Bramley Zion decided to enter. It was probably the first time anyone from the Sunday school league had dared to put his name forward and as a result Alan received a generous handicap. Possibly some of the members of the handicap panel had no idea of the standard of players in the league. Alan was a good competitor and had played for both Bramley Wanderers at football and Pudsey Britannia at cricket.He was older than me and so I never saw him play either game.

After easy wins in the first two rounds, people began to take notice and it was no surprise when Alan reached the semi-final and was drawn to play one of the favourites at the neutral venue of Laisterdyke Working Mens Club near Bradford. Eight of us went from Farsley to support Alan. It was just as well we did as the other chap, from Morley, had brought along a good contingent hoping that common sense would prevail and that this upstart from the Sunday school league would be out-classed. Both sets of supporters applauded some excellent billiards even if, as the evening wore on, the noise level rose. Smithy won but it was close and the general opinion was that the man from Morley (the name Dunning springs to mind) was the better player but could not overcome the handicap he had to concede.

Neither my dad nor I could get to the final at Leeds Tramways Club when Alan's opponent was a guy called Frankie from Huddersfield, the hot favourite and a previous winner. There was a rumour circulating that he had already sold the prize for the winner, a cue and case. At the interval Alan was in front but those allegedly in the know said Frankie was hanging back so the betting odds would improve. I suspect that the betting was illegal but my informant told me he had never seen so many Wesleyans, Methodists and Baptists queuing up to place a bet. They knew that all Alan had to do was to keep it tight and victory would be his. He managed to keep Frankie sitting in his chair and ran out the winner. Alan entered the next year to defend his title but was handicapped out of it but he had had his moment of glory.

Snooker took over as the more popular game, particularly as it came over so well on television and so when Steve Davis was due to play John Higgins at Oulton Sports Centre I decided to watch professional snooker live for the first time. I was very impressed and became a regular visitor to the Barbican Centre in York which was the venue for the UK Championships for several years, with the later stages of the competition being shown on BBC2. While I was lurking in the lobby area I was asked if I would like to ask John Parrott a question live on television. I was not sure but agreed when I was told that time was short and there was no one else. What a good move it was as I was introduced to Hazel Irvine, the BBC TV presenter, who shook my hand which I did not wash for a week. Hazel put me at ease – a charming lady. John Parrott was also very affable and asked what my question was as we would be live on television.

The matches that afternoon were Mark Williams v Stephen Hendrie and Steve Davis v Graeme Dott. I asked John which match to watch as the first would involve a lot of potting and big breaks whilst the other could be more tactical. Off air he said that was a good question and everything went well when we were live. Who was the only person to see my moment of 'fame'? My mother in law – bless her.

I enjoy watching snooker but do not have sufficient enthusiasm to travel further afield.

CHAPTER 6

Watching and Following Football 1946 – 1958

My first recollection of taking an interest in professional football was looking at the results of the various leagues played in the later stages of World War 2. One name stood out for me – Aston Villa. It was not the usual suffix of Town, United or City and where was Aston? My mother said it was a part of Birmingham which was in the Midlands – I got the impression quite clearly that it was too far for a visit now that the Football League started again in season 1946/47.

I noticed that they were due to play at Huddersfield on Boxing Day. My father had been a regular visitor to Leeds Road before the war and, after much nattering from both myself and my mother who wanted a bit of peace and quiet, Dad agreed to take me. I can't remember how we got there – Huddersfield was 15 miles away from Farsley – but I was amazed by the whole experience. A large crowd crammed into the ground and most of them were on the East Terrace with Dad, me and Uncle Cyril. I was pushed to the front so that I could see and told not to move. Unfortunately the bottom step of the terracing was below the level of the pitch and when the ball was on the other side of the field I could not see it as the pitch had a crown in the middle gradually sloping to each touch line. It was odd to see players running about apparently aimlessly and then, suddenly, the ball came into view and it all made sense again.

The bad news for me was that the Huddersfield number 9, Rodgers scored the only goal of the game to give Town victory over my adopted heroes but the disappointment was over-shadowed by the whole atmosphere of the occasion – I was hooked on football.

Huddersfield were not doing very well and only avoided relegation by beating Leeds United with only two matches left. Leeds finished bottom with only 18 points from 42 games and accompanied Brentford into Division 2. Apparently it was not that the Dad was a Town supporter but that Huddersfield was then the only place to see the top teams and players as this was well before the Premier League with wall to wall TV. Stanley Matthews (Blackpool), Tom Finney (Preston) and Wilf Mannion (Middlesbrough) not forgetting Peter Doherty, Vic Metcalfe and Jimmy Glazzard, all of Huddersfield, could only be seen live -. as could the mighty Arsenal, Manchester United, Burnley and Derby County.

In 1948 I left primary school and went to Bradford Grammar School. The significance of this might have affected my footballing allegiance as the trolley bus from the city centre to school went down Manningham Lane and passed Valley Parade, the home of Bradford City who seemed rooted in Division 3 (North). My mother decreed it was too far for a 10 year old to go to Huddersfield but could not see a problem with Bradford as, after all, it was just like going to school. The crowds were not as big as at Huddersfield and I did tell my mother that half our form would also be there. This was somewhat of an exaggeration as I was going alone but felt the end justified the means.

Instead of Peter Doherty and Vic Metcalfe, it was Andy McGill who performed a ritual dance between some swords with a piper in attendance prior to the match, Jock Whyte and Eddie Carr. Not forgetting a former Town player, Bill Price, who on one infamous occasion, missed two penalties in successive minutes at the City end. In another memorable match, against Rotherham, City were leading 3-1 and contrived to lose 4-3 in a thrilling finish.

In 1950 there was a fundamental and final decision as to my football allegiance with the initial stages taking place at Farsley Parish Church. One of my fellow choristers was Dudley Williams, whose ambition was to play on the right wing for Huddersfield Town. His parents decided otherwise and after a distinguished academic career he became a professor commanding huge fees for lectures, particularly in America, as well as Oxford and Cambridge However, what is far more important is that Dudley's dad worked at Crofts Engineers at Thornbury from where he organised a coach trip to Leeds Road each home match. At the time virtually everyone worked on a Saturday morning and so the coach left Crofts at 12.30 or so, calling for refreshments at a pub in Brighouse and then on to the game. The added bonus was that the

Farsley Parish Church Choir 1947
Dudley Williams – front row third from left,
John Hudson – back row extreme right
The author front row second from right

coach depot was in Stanningley, not far from our house, and so Dudley and I were transported more or less door to door – the cost (reduced for children) of one shilling and three pence was peanuts and in any case, my mother paid.

In season 1950/51, the highlights came in the FA Cup.Round 3 brought the mighty Tottenham Hotspur to Leeds Road with their famous 'push and run' team managed by Arthur Rowe. As usual, unfortunately, Town were struggling near the foot of the table while Spurs were riding high and eventually won the First Division Championship. On a very wet day which kept the attendance down to just over 25,000, it was the underdogs who came out on top. Town's scorers were Jeff Taylor and Jimmy Glazzard in a 2-0 win, earning a trip to Preston North End whose star was Tom Finney, an England international.

With Town clinging on to a slender 1-0 lead through a Vic Metcalfe penalty, Preston were awarded a spot kick and up stepped Tom Finney. Jack Wheeler, Town's goalkeeper, had broken his arm and was 'helping out and being a nuisance on the right wing' – no substitutes in those days – and so it was Harold Hassall who stood between the posts. No doubt the Preston supporters thought the equaliser was on the way but Harold anticipated in which corner of the goal the ball was going and made a superb save. Not only that, but he punted the ball downfield and it bounced over the Preston centre half, Mattinson, for Jeff Taylor to run on to score the goal which ensured Town's epic victory. In the 5th round a trip to Wolverhampton saw a 2-nil defeat and the cup run was over.

Although Town finished in 19th place in Division 1, satisfaction could be drawn from the fact that they defeated the champions Spurs, not only in the FA Cup, but also twice in the league winning 3-2 at home and 2-0 at White Hart Lane with Jimmy Glazzard scoring in all three games.

The next season Town also beat the eventual champions, Manchester United, 3-2 at Leeds Road but that could not conceal the disappointment at being relegated from the top flight for the first time. While in the end Stoke City had a three point cushion over Town, there was drama at White Hart Lane when a mistake as to the laws of the game by the referee denied Town what at the time was a vital point. Eddie Bailey took a corner kick; the ball struck the referee and rebounded to Bailey who crossed for Len Duquemin to head home the 'winner' for Spurs. Despite a Football League enquiry, the result was allowed to stand. Just consider what would happen now if, in similar circumstances to Town, Manchester United were involved and as a result stood to lose out on the Championship. Manager Andy Beattie had been appointed just before the end of the season when relegation was inevitable but for the start of 1952/53 brought with him from Stockport County Ron Staniforth, a full back who later won international honours with England, and Tommy Cavanagh a hard working inside forward. Jimmy Watson from Motherwell was also recruited and these three players were to have a big influence on the side.

This was a season for records. The back six – goalkeeper, two full backs and three half backs- remained unchanged in all 42 league games. Vic Metcalfe, on the left wing, was also an ever-present. Town also had their highest average league attendance – 27,764. This was a reflection not only of Town's success on the pitch but also the fact that there were several local derbies. Unfortunately I missed the highlight of the season when a 2-1 defeat at Everton was avenged in style with an 8-2 victory at Leeds Road the following day. Jimmy Glazzard headed four goals all from crosses by Vic Metcalfe.

Town finished as runners-up to Sheffield United and some pundits, when promotion had been achieved, said that relegation had proved to be a blessing in forcing the club to re-group. The spectators also appreciated watching a winning team rather one continually struggling in Division 1. However the platform had been laid and Town finished the next season (1953/54) in third place behind Wolves and West Brom. Town did the double over Liverpool who were relegated after finishing bottom of the league.

For me, the FA Cup run provided the highlights of the next season. Coventry City, from a lower division, gave Town a fright at Leeds Road in a 3-3 draw and I was pleased when the ref blew the final whistle. This brought a 5th round visit to second division Liverpool with the media expecting an upset. Billy Liddell, a Scottish international, was the star for the Anfield men but he was well held by Ken Taylor and Town ran out 2-0 winners. I stood on the Kop wearing my blue and white scarf, walked down Scotland Road to the city centre and lived to tell the tale. In all the years of watching football, this was the most satisfying match of all.

In the 6th round Town were leading 1-0 in the closing minutes when Jimmy Glazzard was pushed to the ground in the penalty box by a Newcastle United defender. Penalty!! No, the ref waved play on and Bobby Mitchell shimmied his way down the left wing on the grandstand side and crossed the ball for Len White, later to star for Town, to head home the equaliser. This was daylight robbery and United not only won the replay but the FA Cup final.

Wins in the last two games took Town to 12th position but the ominous signs were there and next season Town struggled and despite winning the last four matches finished in 21st place and relegation to Division 2. The match I recall in a disappointing season was the 4-0 victory over Sunderland who were spending money as if it were going out of fashion. There was also a good win against Blackpool who finished up as runners-up to Manchester United

In November 1956 I started my two year stint in the army – national service was compulsory. I remember watching a local derby between Aldershot and Reading and when I got a permanent posting to Bicester there were regular visits to London and the Midlands as the main railway line to the North West, from Paddington to Birkenhead, passed through the town. Wolves and Arsenal were the teams to watch. Reduced rail fares and admission to football matches made for a pleasant afternoon. I remember Arsenal scoring five goals against a Birmingham City side who were dire.

I managed to get to see Town at West Ham in November 1957 when we went down 5-2; it was too far to the Valley where, after leading 5-1, Town lost 7-6 to Charlton on December 21st – what a Christmas present.

CHAPTER 7

Watching and Following Football The 1960's

During this decade, I was either playing or refereeing and so I did not see as many matches as I would have liked. Huddersfield Town, after being relegated in 1956 were to spend 14 years in Division 2 before returning to their rightful spot in the top echelon of English football. I was very disappointed that we were not competing against Arsenal and Newcastle but now, in 2009, I would gladly settle for a spell in the second tier or the Championship as it is now called.

How much worse it might have been! With four games to go in 1961 Town seemed doomed to relegation to Division 3 which was unthinkable but three of those games were won and disaster averted. The highlight of that season was the installation of the Denis Law floodlights – so called because the money came the sale of the brilliant inside forward to Manchester City. After battling for a draw at Wolves, the current leaders of Division 1, there was a race against time to get the floodlights ready for the replay in which Town were given little chance. You only get one bite at the cherry. When Derek Stokes put Town ahead, hopes were high. Murray equalised for wolves and up stepped Mike O'Grady to slot home the winner at the Cowshed end for the winner. A crowd of over 40,000, four times the average gate, braved a bitterly cold night but went home ecstatic.

Barnsley were awaiting the winners and another massive crowd were at Leeds Road hoping for another floodlight fiesta. Duncan Sharp, displaying all the fighting qualities of the TV character played by Blades fan Sean Bean was a rock at the heart of the visitors defence and it took a John Coddington penalty to earn Town a draw.The replay at Oakwell was played on the following Wednesday afternoon and I took a day of my annual holiday entitlement to be there. Unfortunately, Wood, the Barnsley right half scored the only goal of the game and I travelled home in the rain with the weather matching my mood. At least we could concentrate on the league which we really needed to do.

In the next few seasons Town's league form improved and in 1966 featured on Match of the Day in the final game against Coventry City but went down 2-0 and hopes of promotion were dashed.

In this decade the highlights were in the FA Cup. Following the drama against Wolves and Barnsley, there was an inglorious 5-0 defeat at Old Trafford. This third round tie, scheduled to be played in early January, was postponed quite a number of times in view of the wintry conditions and eventually took place on 4th March. One of my work colleagues had a car and we travelled 'over the hill'. Progress was slow – no M62 in those days – and as we got to the turnstile there was a huge roar. We thought that was for the teams coming out. When we got to a place where we could see on the terrace, Denis Law, back from Italy, scored what prove to be the second United goal and by the time we had digested that bad news more was to follow. He scored again and later completed his hat-trick. Was our journey really necessary? The return trip was not too bad following a couple of pints of bitter.

The following season Chelsea were beaten at Stamford Bridge with Kevin McHale and Len White getting the goals in a 2-1 win. I had been playing football that afternoon and could hardly believe the score when I got home.

In 1967/68 season it was the Football League Cup which provided the excitement when Town reached the semi-final. Victories over Wolves, Norwich and West Ham and a draw at Fulham brought the men from Craven Cottage back to Leeds Road for a replay. When the match went into extra time, I had to make a decision. If I stayed I would have to walk from Shipley to Menston as the last bus would have gone. David Shaw made my long trek home up Hollins Hill well worthwhile by scoring the winner. A few weeks later I saw Les Wood who lived in Menston and he asked whether I had been to the Fulham replay. It turned out that he had been to the game with Gerry Butler and they had passed me in Gerry's car but were not sure it was me and didn't stop. The euphoria of victory eased the disappointment.

The semi-final against Arsenal was over two legs. By this time I was working with a company in Bradford called Flexicon and when the Sales Director suggested that he and I should visit our three branches in London, I came up with 17th January. Yes, the date for the first leg at Highbury. Our Area Manager got the tickets, booked the hotel and, as they say, the job was a good un. Colin Dobson got a late goal to make the score 2-3 to Arsenal but this made for an exciting second leg in a fortnight's time. Tony Leighton put Town in front at Leeds Road and technically we were in front on the away goals rule, however the Gunners hit back with three goals and ran out deserved winners.

The last three games of 1968/1969 were won and how often a team which ends a season strongly starts well next time. After 14 years in what some supporters termed the 'wilderness' Town returned to the top flight by topping the Second Division by seven points when a win was two points and not three as at present. Season 1969/1970 which started in the sixties ended the decade in style.

In the early part of the decade, I was working with Midland Bank in Bradford and at that time Burnley had a good side and qualified to play in Europe. Blacklaw was in goal, the full backs were Angus and Elder, the half backs Adamson, Cummings and Miller with a forward line of Connelly, McIlroy, Pointer, Robson and Pilkington. Wardways Coaches used to run trips to Turf Moor starting from The Alhambra Theatre in Morley Street and I was a regular together with some of my work colleagues. The Clarets played Rheims who had Raymond Kopa in their forward line – he got no change out of the Burnley defence.

There were also some exciting cup replays and Tuesday nights were something special. Fortunately the coach used to arrive back in Bradford just in time for a pint before catching the last bus home – number 90.

Having made the trip to Old Trafford for the Huddersfield cup tie, my appetite was whetted for more games there and my friend at Crompton Parkinson Philip (sorry his surname escapes me) was willing to drive his ancient sports car. I remember a European match against Spurs when Dave Mackay broke his leg but even after that tragedy, the quality of football was scintillating.

A combination of getting married and changing jobs brought those trips to an end but I shall always remember Philip's comment once on the way back when, in the middle of nowhere and going at a fair speed, he said his car went better on Tetley's bitter than Esso – I have never tasted Esso but I took Philip's word for it.

CHAPTER 8

The Depression of the 1970's

Although this decade started and ended in triumph, this period must go down as the worst in Town's history. After seeing Steve Smith's goal at Middlesbrough clinch promotion and then win the Division with victories over Blackburn and Watford, I was confident that we could do well on our return to the top flight. Indeed, when we beat Blackpool and Southampton at home and sat proudly at the top of the league everything was rosy.I managed to see both games as the cricket was rained off for the first match and the second was mid-week. However the fixture away at Liverpool brought a few home truths with a thumping 4-0 defeat. I was playing cricket and arranged for our scorer to have his radio handy so he could keep me up to date – we lost at cricket as well.

That defeat started a run of nine games without a win and we then all knew it would be a survival battle to avoid a quick return to 'the wilderness'. The problem was the inability to score goals at home – only 19 in 21 games. With only 16 conceded Leeds Road was not the place for a goal fest.

The outstanding match of the season was on January 16th when Arsenal, later to be crowned champions, were the visitors. A Frank Worthington penalty for handball against Frank McLintock put Town ahead at the Cowshed end only for Arsenal to hit back with an equaliser following intense pressure. In the second half Les Chapman got possession of the ball just inside the Arsenal half, surged forward and smashed a terrific shot into the top corner giving Bob Wilson no chance – for me it was the goal of the season and has been shown many times since on television. I understand this was Arsenal's last defeat of the season as they went on to pip one of the other West Yorkshire teams by a point. Three points from the last two games at Spurs and West Ham made the final position of 15th a little flattering.

It was clear that the team needed a bit more quality but the only significant transfer was the sale of Jimmy McGill. The writing was on the wall with no win until the seventh match of the season.

Town finished bottom of the league and the statistics were so depressing that I shall not compound my own misery by repeating them.

The one comparative bright spot to the season was the FA Cup run when after beating Burnley, Fulham and West Ham (featured on Match of the Day), Town went down 3-1 at Birmingham. The key incident was when Bob Latchford, the Birmingham centre forward, crashed into David Lawson who had to leave the field. With an emergency goalkeeper Town struggled with Trevor Cherry's goal coming too late to affect the result. Nowadays I am sure Bob Latchford would have been sent off and of course, Town would have had a substitute goalkeeper.

There was transfer drama in the close season with Cherry and Ellam going to Leeds and Worthington to Leicester. Coming in were Alan Gowling and Graham Pugh, two players who might have saved Town from relegation the previous season, had they been signed earlier. Particularly Alan Gowling who scored 17 goals in yet another depressing relegation albeit this time on goal average

After 63 years as a full member of the Football League, Town found themselves in unfamiliar territory. Visits to Rochdale, Shrewsbury and Southport did not have much glamour but the slide was halted and a final position of 10th was deemed by some to be satisfactory even if it was one below Halifax Town.

However the youth team reached the final of the FA Youth Cup only to be beaten by a strong Spurs side in extra time at Leeds Road. The crowd of 15,000 showed the desperation for any success – this was almost three times the average for the season.

The mention of Spurs brings to mind a match at Elland Road. I was standing on the Lowfields Road side and with Leeds losing by the odd goal and with not long to go, Allan Clarke had the ball just outside the Spurs penalty area. Not wishing to lose possession he went one way and then the other. This provoked one supporter to shout 'Shoot Clarke' – another spectator with a sense of humour replied 'Why pick on Clarke?' Terrace side wit at its best.

The atmosphere was very different when United met West Brom at Elland Road in a match which on the football coupons was a home banker. The visitors won with a disputed goal; Tony Brown, the Albion mid-fielder who scored a lot of goals going forward to link with Jeff Astle the centre forward, was returning from an offside position when the ball was played forward towards him. Was he interfering with play? or had he got back onside before the ball was kicked ?. Referee Ray Tinkler of Boston decided everything was OK and waved play on while the linesman had his flag in the air. The Leeds defenders looked on in amazement and when the ball was crossed from the right, Jeff Astle was able to take his time and tapped the ball past the goalkeeper. Would the current interpretation of the offside law have made any difference? Another issue involved the goal scorer – was he offside? Certainly he would have had to have been behind the ball when it was passed to him as there was only one Leeds player, the keeper, within 30 yards. The linesman could not see because he was out of position after the previous incident in mid-field.

The crowd, already frustrated at the score line, was incensed and invaded the pitch. Eventually the match resumed but as a result of the crowd behaviour, Leeds had to play some 'home' matches away from Elland Road. I remember two at Leeds Road and one at Hull.

In the summer of 1974 Ian Greaves resigned and Bobby Collins was appointed – his first managerial post. Season 1974/1975 has to be the nadir in Town's history. Despite Alan Gowling's usual high quota of goals, Town ended up bottom of the pile, six points (three wins) away from safety. I have no worthwhile memories of this season.

The first season in the basement division brought a change to Leeds Road – our team were challenging for promotion. With four matches to go the Waterhouse family travelled en masse to Prenton Park for the vital game against Tranmere. We set off early because our two daughters wanted to go on the ferry across the Mersey- not any ferry but the one shown in the opening titles of the Liver Birds, a popular TV programme at that time, when Nerys Hughes lost her hat.

With mission accomplished we went on to the game.

A quick resume is as follows:

We lost 3-0
Ronnie Moore fell down in the box three times
The referee gave three penalties
Promotion push over.

We missed out on promotion by two points in fifth place – no prizes for guessing who got the last promotion place in fourth position.

The next season saw seven consecutive wins between 22nd January and 12th March but a poor finish meant a ninth place finish, nine points off promotion.

1977/1978 saw Town finish in their lowest position ever – 11th in Division 4. This improved by two places next season but significantly Mick Buxton was now in charge and a strong finish augured well. My memory, probably the only one in yet another poor season, was the 3-0 thrashing given to some upstarts from Wimbledon

As with the 1960s, the decade ended in triumph – whoever said the only way was up must have had Town in mind in the 1970's

CHAPTER 9

The 1980's – Better Times

What a start to Season 1979/1980 – in the first twelve matches, there were 10 wins, one draw and only one defeat. The double was completed over Wigan Athletic and Port Vale were thumped 7-1 at Leeds Road. Match no 11 was Peterborough United away and fired with enthusiasm I decided to drive down the A1 to see the game. Elder daughter Karen, 14 years old at the time, came with me while her younger sister Jane (13) went shopping with her mummy.

We arrived in Peterborough at lunch time and all the coffee bars and cafes were full. Reluctantly we had to take refreshment at the Bull Hotel with Karen under strict instructions not to tell her mother. Ian Robbins scored twice and Peter Fletcher added a third for a 3-1 win for Town.

After a great day out we arrived home and Jane, no doubt trying to get one over on her sister made a point of showing off a new dress. Karen, never one at being backward to come forward, responded by saying 'Yes, but we had our lunch in a posh pub in Peterborough'. Fortunately Sandra saw the funny side even when Karen added that she had had a sip of Daddy's beer.

Just before Christmas there was a rumour that Town were going to sign a big name forward. On 21st December Rochdale were thrashed 5-1 and we wondered what all the fuss was about. However Steve Kindon signed on the dotted line and scored 14 goals in the second half of the season and with Ian Robbins netting 25 and Peter Fletcher 17, Town amassed 101 league goals a record for the club. And to think that the season started in the depressing 1970s.

Just as the season had got off to a good start, the finish was also impressive. Of the last 13 games, Town were unbeaten with 9 wins and 4 draws. In a season of highlights I particularly remember Steve Kindon's late late equaliser at Walsall and the 4-0 thrashing of York City at Bootham Crescent which certainly gave me the bragging rights at work.

Life in Division 3 did not start well with no wins in the first four games; but in another excellent season, Town finished in fourth place just three points behind Charlton Athletic who got the last promotion spot. The particular highlights for me were the match against Barnsley when a crowd of 28, 901 saw a Dave Cowling header at the Cowshed end, enough to see off our local rivals and the long trip to The Valley where goals from Malcolm Brown and Steve Kindon gave Town a 2-1 win.

Season 1981/1982 saw Town slump to 17th position mainly to injuries which ended the carers of Fred Robinson, Steve Kindon, Peter Fletcher and goalkeepers Richard Taylor and Andy Rankin. After the goal scoring exploits of previous seasons, no Town player reached double figures. However this was to lead to better things the following season.

With a new strike force of Mark Lillis and Colin Russell Town gained promotion to Division 2 by finishing in third place four points in front of Newport County who were defeated at Leeds Road 1-0 on 7th May with only two matches to go. A Dave Cowling left foot drive, again at the Cowshed end did the business for Town. The highlight of a reasonable run in the League Cup was at Elland Road on 10th November 1982 when a near post header by Dave Cowling was enough to beat Leeds United 1-0. For several years Cowling Day was celebrated in the Waterhouse household. There was also an outstanding performance from Brian Stanton on New Year's Day when he scored four goals as Town beat Bradford City 6-3.

CHAPTER 10

Mid Eighties in Division 2

For the next four seasons Town held their own in Division 2 after promotion. Two quality players were brought in: Brian Laws, a hard tackling full- back from Burnley and the cultured centre-half Paul Jones from Bolton. After a good start with three wins and three draws in the first six matches, Town fell away. None of the first ten matches in the New Year brought a win and the final league position of 12th was satisfactory in the circumstances bearing in mind that the promoted clubs were Chelsea, Sheffield Wednesday and Newcastle United, with Manchester City just missing out. This was to be Town's best finish for some time dropping down to 13th, 16th and 17th before a disastrous relegation season in 1987/1988.

The outstanding memory was the Easter Monday trip to Maine Road, when, after Dave Sutton in the first minute had to go off injured, Town played magnificently to win 3-2; this just pipped the Boxing Day victory at Elland Road when the Lillis/Russell duo brought a 2-1 win.

The next season saw Sam Allardyce arrive together with Dale Tempest. Following a poor start, Town won eight and drew one in a nine match spell from mid October to December and hopes were high. However in the final 10 matches there was only one win. One remarkable and most unfortunate statistic involved the two matches against Shrewsbury Town who won on both occasions 5-1 and, as the saying goes, I was there. With Town struggling near the foot of the table in March, Duncan Shearer was signed from Chelsea. In his first match he scored a hat-trick at Barnsley and went on to add another four before the end of the season. Relegation was avoided by six points (two wins).

1986/1987 saw Town at the foot of the table in mid December and Mick Buxton, who had managed Town's rise from fourth Division obscurity was dismissed; Steve Smith took over.

Victories in the last three games ensured safety which owed much to Duncan Shearer's haul of 21 league goals.

While 1974/1975 remains, in my opinion, as the worst season I can remember, 1987/1988 was worse statistically but was played in a higher division. It was not until the 15th game of the season that Town recorded a win by which time Steve Smith had been succeeded by the flamboyant Malcolm McDonald. Hindsight is a wonderful thing but whatever logic there was to the appointment defied belief. Relegation was confirmed long before the end of the season with the final margin of 'safety' a massive 19 points. I witnessed humiliation at Maine Road on 7th November when Town were beaten 10-1. Some defenders thought we were playing an offside trap but others didn't. The result was chaos and to make matters worse Town wore the unpopular strip of black and yellow squares. The journey back over the foggy hills was depressing to say the least.

Next season Eoin Hand stopped the rot thanks to a hatful of goals from Craig Maskell who had been signed as replacement for Duncan Shearer, Town finished in 14th and then 8th position in the league to end the 1980s. April 1st 1989 may have been April Fool's Day but it was Bury who suffered to the tune of 6-0.However a year later the score line was reversed – not a day to remember. In the FA Cup Town reached the fourth round and we all went to Selhurst Park in high spirits on the back of a run of five wins and two draws in the league but were crushed 4-0 by a Palace side who were far too good on the day. The result spoiled what could have been a good trip – the lunch and entertainment (Bob 'The 'Cat' Bevan was hilarious) were superb. When we got back to West Yorkshire it was snowing and the last few miles home made it into a long and unhappy day.

Earlier in the 1989/1990 season, Town performed well in the Littlewoods Challenge Cup. Having been held to a draw at Leeds Road by Doncaster, they went to Belle Vue and won 2-1 thanks to two goals from Robert Wilson. When the draw for the next round was made Town had a tie against Nottingham Forest who at the time were one of the top teams in the country. For the first leg at the City Ground I went on a VIP trip which included a meal before the game. Due to heavy traffic on the M1 we arrived late and had to take our seats before we had had our pudding. The catering manager was somewhat concerned and promised that we could return to the restaurant after the match to finish our meal. Ken O'Doherty scored for Town in a 1-1 draw and we really enjoyed our bread and butter pudding and complimentary cup of coffee before catching the coach back to Huddersfield. With away goals counting double in the event of the aggregate scores being level, Town were in the driving seat. Forest cared not a jot and with fifteen minutes to go were leading 3-1 but late goals from Craig Maskell and Mike Cecere made it 3-3 after 90 minutes. Forest used their European experience to hang on and won the tie on the away goals rule. They went on to win the trophy.

In the following summer I was watching Yorkshire play Nottinghamshire at cricket at Scarborough and sitting in front of me was a party from Nottingham who from time to time mentioned football and so I posed the following question to them. Which team did Forest not beat when they won the Littlewoods Challenge Cup last season ? Eventually one of their group realised what I was getting at but his teenage daughter thought hard and long before the penny dropped.

CHAPTER 11

The Early Nineties

The main change in personnel for the start of the 1990/1991 season was the signing of Iwan Roberts from Watford for £275,000 (a club record) to replace Craig Maskell, a prolific goal-scorer in the previous three campaigns, who moved on to Swindon Town. Iwan, after a slow start, managed 13 league goals with midfielder Kieran O'Regan chipping in with 11. But this did include 8 from the penalty spot.

Town made their first live TV appearance in the FA Cup tie at Altrincham – no doubt an upset was expected by someone. However, goals from Iffy Onuora and Iwan Roberts gave Town a 2-1 win. The second round tie was delayed due to bad weather; this created more interest as the winners had been drawn to play Spurs at home in the third round. Unfortunately Blackpool won 2-0 at Leeds Road and the opportunity of a money spinning match against the side from North London was lost.

Town finished in 11th position, six points away from a play off place following a disappointing end to the season with no victories in the last five games.

The following season was far more eventful. Iwan Roberts scored 34 goals in all competitions and with 24 of those coming in the league won the Adidas/Shoot Golden Shoe Award for being the joint leading goal scorer in the Division. The FA Cup provided two records; the 7-0 victory over Lincoln United was Town's biggest home win in the competition whilst the 4-0 defeat to Millwall was the largest home defeat.

An impressive run of seven wins and a draw in the last eight matches lifted Town into third position and a place in the play -offs for the first time. After a 2-2 draw at London Road in the first leg, hopes were high particularly when Phil Starbuck put Town ahead with an early goal at the open end but Peterborough came back well in the second half to win 2-1. They beat Stockport in the final to clinch promotion after finishing in sixth place.

Earlier in the season Town and Bury provided another high scoring contest. After half an hour Town trailed by four goals, however they pulled one back just before half time and then two more, but in injury time Town were still losing 4-3 when Simon Ireland got away down the right, crossed the ball for Iwan Roberts to head home the equaliser in front of the delirious Town fans massed behind the goal at that end.

There was another notable feat in the league cup then sponsored by Rumbelows; having beaten Sunderland 2-1 at Roker Park thanks to goals by Phil Starbuck and Simon Charlton (was it really a cross which deceived the keeper on a windy night ?), Town thrashed the Black Cats 4-0 at Leeds Road.

Ian Ross had moved up from assistant manager following the departure of Eoin Hand in March and inspired Town in the final flourish to the league programme.

The next season started badly with five straight defeats and with only a third of the season left, former manager Mick Buxton was brought in to help Ian Ross. This produced a dramatic effect; twelve of the last 16 matches were won and after being 10 points from safety Town had a margin of 13 points at the end of the season. Even so 15th place, after all the hopes and expectations following the previous season, was extremely disappointing and, of course, it could have been disastrous.

A reasonable FA Cup run ended in a home defeat at the hands of Southend United in the fourth round with one of the Shrimpers goals being scored by a young Stan Colleymore. Whilst in the Autoglass Trophy, Town were knocked out by Wigan in the Northern Group semi-final.

There was drama in the Rumbelows Cup when, after beating Sunderland on the away goals rule in the first round, Town met high flying Blackburn Rovers. In the first leg at Leeds Road it took a late equaliser from Alan Shearer to make it 1-1; for the second leg I, unfortunately had a business meeting in Leeds. One of the hotel staff said we were drawing well into the second half and when I eventually I got to my car I found there was live commentary on the radio as the match was in extra time. Shortly afterwards Blackburn scored and although Town pressed for the equaliser, it was not to be. The commentators who normally favour the top division sides were full of praise for Town's skill and effort.

CHAPTER 12

The Warnock Era

Neil Warnock was appointed manager in July 1993 and resigned in June 1995 – a period of less than two years. The definition of an era is a long and distinct period of time, however I think in this case one out of two is good enough. A trip to Wembley for the first time in 56 years was followed by another the next season when Town recorded their first victory at the famous stadium at the fifth attempt.

The season started slowly in the league with only one win in the first eight games but in the last twelve matches Town were unbeaten. Winning eight and drawing four; this successful run saw Town finish in eleventh position.

Drama came in the cup competitions. In the second round of the Coca Cola Cup Town drew the mighty Arsenal. In the first leg at Leeds Road the Gunners showed their class and thrashed Town 5-0. In the bar after the game I was standing next to Steve Bould and Tony Adams and, needless to say, let them get served first. At five feet eight inches I felt like a midget. Iain Dunn scored at Highbury in the second leg to earn a 1-1 draw but it was a case of too little too late.

The Autoglass Trophy, a competition not taken too seriously by some clubs, provided Town with success which gave the players confidence. The result being an unbeaten league run in towards the end of the season. After getting past Doncaster and Rotherham, Town drew Preston North End at home on a bitterly cold November evening. After 120 minutes the score was still 0-0 and we entered into a penalty shoot out at the Cowshed End. I had to keep calm as I was doing the Video commentary but with my position on the gantry rapidly becoming like Ice Station Zebra, Town came out on top 5-4.

The next match, against Crewe, went into extra time but goals from Phil Starbuck (2) and Andy Booth gave Town a 3-2 win to earn the dubious pleasure of a trip to Stockport who, after the draw had been made, walloped Town 3-0 at Edgeley Park. I travelled on the Supporters Club coach more in hope than expectation on that cool but clear evening. In the first forty five minutes, we never looked as if we would be beaten and I was surprised when the gentleman on the PA system advertised coach trips to Carlisle for the next round during the interval. I doubt whether the Town players heard this but they tore into County in the second half. The goal came after the ball had been pinging around in the six yard box similar to a pin ball machine when Iain Dunn got control and knocked it into the roof of the net. Roared on by a good following of supporters in a crowd of just less than 5,000, Town were not going to lose this one and held out for an unexpected, but well deserved, victory.

The first leg of the Northern Area Final against Carlisle United was played at Leeds Road and Town romped home 4-1. Little did we realise that late goal from Iain (he ain't got no hair but we don't care) Dunn would prove to be so important. Sandra and I decided to have an overnight stay in Carlisle for the second leg and found a good B & B near to Brunton Park; not surprisingly it was run by a Carlisle supporter. With the away goals rule applying to this competition, alarms bells were ringing when the home side scored two goals. One more would win the tie for them unless Town could score one themselves which seemed unlikely at the time. Finally after some eight minutes of injury time played, the referee blew his whistle and the cry of 'Wembley here we come' rang out loudly from the jubilant fans into the Cumbrian night. We celebrated well but had to be careful as both teams play in blue and white; fortunately the atmosphere was good and there were no problems.

The next morning we were looking round the city centre when Sandra, a keen knitter, spotted some wool at a bargain price. The lady in the shop was quite chatty and asked how long we were staying. When we said we had come for the football match, she twigged which team we supported and jokingly threatened to double the price. She wished us well for the final and I think she meant it.

The shirt is wearing well

Tony Hobson and some of his friends from Harrogate suggested we organise a coach for the Wembley trip and after many telephone calls we managed to fill a 54 seater which would start from Harrogate, picking up at Wetherby on the way. Leicester Forest East was a sea of blue and white with 30,000 town fans travelling down – not all of them were at the services area but it seemed like it at the time.

Richard Logan equalised an early Swansea goal with one of the best headers I have seen but eventually Town lost out on penalties; still it was a good day out.

The last first team match was played at the historic Leeds Road ground on April 30th 1994 when many tears were shed. Phil Starbuck scored the winner at the open end to give Town a 2-1 win over Blackpool with over 16,000 determined to pay their respects.

Many Town supporters were looking forward to 1994/1995 in view of the tremendous end to the previous season and with the sun shining at Blackpool on 13th August the promenade was literally a sea of blue and white by late morning. Surprisingly the match was not all-ticket despite, I understand, a request from the Town club. There were some crowd problems as the area allocated to away supporters quickly filled up and latecomers infiltrated the other parts of the ground. Fortunately the police sorted things out and the game got under way. Paul Reid opened the scoring and added another later and sandwiched in between were two from 'Rocket' Ronnie Jepson. 4-1 away in the first match within the second at the new McAlpine Stadium – bring on Wycombe was the cry.

The trip to Blackpool brought back some memories; we had a snack lunch at the Cliffs Hotel where Sandra and I spent our honeymoon and on the way back to Bloomfield Road we passed Uncle Tom's Cabin. When the children were old enough to appreciate a seaside holiday we booked in at a small hotel which provided a baby sitting service and so one evening we set off towards the hotspots of Blackpool. It started raining when we were passing Uncle Tom's Cabin and decided that would be our first port of call.. The place was heaving and when a white coated waiter offered to bring our drinks into the concert room, what else could we do but agree. The first 'turn' was a female singer whose main asset was not her voice but her huge chest; things improved when a short fat bloke with a Lancashire accent started with his comedy patter. Sandra was laughing away at some of the jokes which were a darker shade of blue. I found this a little strange as her nickname used by her father was 'prim'. When I made some remark about enjoying herself, the quick response was 'I can laugh because nobody knows me here'

In all the excitement the Chief Executive, Paul Fletcher, commented quietly that home teams playing in a new ground for the first time generally lost. How right he was and the Wycombe goal was scored by none other than Simon Garner who had caused Town pain in the past when playing for Blackburn.

The next match was at Chester and once again the Waterhouse clan travelled in force. Andy Booth got the first goal and then Iain Dunn scored the winner for a Town victory 2-1. The Booth/Jepson partnership blossomed as the season progressed with Boothy netting 26 goals and Rocket Ronnie 19.

Apart from the Wycombe defeat, Town remained unbeaten until 5th November when they crashed 3-0 at, of all places, York City. Monday morning at work was not pleasant. Fortunately in the return match at the McAlpine, the score was reversed.

It was clear Town meant business when, in December, they signed Lee Duxbury and Lee Sinnott from rivals Bradford City for a reported combined fee of £500,000.

A disappointing 1-0 defeat at Hull on Boxing Day meant Town had gone 4 matches without a win but Andy Booth got the only goal of the game the next day against Rotherham at home and the tide turned. With seven games to go, Town were challenging for the one automatic promotion spot but only six out of a possible 21 points were won and that meant fifth place and the last play off spot.

The two legs against Brentford both ended up 1-1 and so Town faced a penalty shoot out. Listening on the radio was agonising as after each penalty there was a great roar from the crowd and the seconds it took for the commentator to say what had happened seemed an eternity But the noise that greeted the spot kick taken by Darren Bullock was such that we were in no doubt that he had scored and once again 'Wembley here we come' rang out loud and clear from the Town faithful who had made the long mid-week trek to London. The ecstasy of victory was tempered by the fact that I should have been there.

A few evenings later I came home from playing tennis to find that Sandra and Tony Hobson had organised a coach for the Wembley trip; this time with Sykes Coaches of Appleton Roebuck.I suppose it would have been magical to have got on a bus at the end of our road straight to Wembley but logistically this was not possible and we drove to Wetherby as before. I organised a quiz and the journey down passed quickly.

Andy Booth scored at the end further away from us and then Marcus Stewart, later to sign for Town, equalised just before half time. With less than ten minutes to go Iain Dunn who had come on as a sub took a free kick from the inside left position and Boothy nodded the ball back from outside the far post for Chris Billy to head home the winner. Town were back into the second tier of English football.

The cup competitions did not bring too much excitement except for round two of the Autoglass Windscreen Shield when Iain Dunn created history by being the first player to score the winning goal on a 'sudden death' basis. At the time it was called the Golden Goal and a few weeks later Iain received a trophy to commemorate the feat. How about that for a quiz question?

CHAPTER 13

Back in the Second Tier of English Football

If consolidation was the aim, expectations were exceeded when Town finished in eighth position. New manager Brian Horton, who had quite a bit of experience at this level, brought in Paul Dalton, Steve Jenkins and Lee Makel. Later in the season Rob Edwards was signed from Crewe and he scored the winner on his debut against Luton Town. Andy Booth and Ronnie Jepson continued the good work with both getting into double figures for league goals.

Sunderland won the Division and when we travelled to Roker Park on 30th March, a hard game was expected. After a walk on the sea front, a couple of pints and some fish and chips, our family was well prepared. At half time the score was 1-1 but as the players were coming off the field Ben Thornley was having a heated discussion with the referee and he did not re-appear after the interval. Town continued to play well and when Andy Booth scored we sensed a victory for the magnificent ten. However with minutes ticking away, Sunderland introduced a young centre forward by the name of Michael Bridges who in the last eight minutes headed two goals at our end of the field. As we made our way back to our car some of the home supporters commiserated with us, maybe that helped but we were still gutted.

In the FA Cup Town beat Blackpool and Peterborough and drew top division side Wimbledon in the fifth round at home. The Dons' tactics seemed to upset some of the aristocrats in the league with their vigorous approach. Town were not fazed and, with the game into injury time, were leading 2-1 when a needless corner was conceded at the Cow Shed End. Maybe I am a pessimist but I said to Sandra 'Oh no, I fear the worst here.'

The ball came over right on the head of Efan Ekoku who planted it in the top corner giving Steve Francis no chance in the Town goal. The game was featured on television in the evening and the commentator had remarked how unlucky we would be if a goal was scored from the corner. C'est la vie!!

In the Coca Cola Cup a 3-1 win at Vale Park in the second leg brought a tie against Barnsley in round two. Simon Collins and Andy Booth scored the goals to give Town a two goal advantage for the second leg at Oakwell. On a wet and windy evening Karen and I set off in good time but such was the volume of traffic that we only got to the ground just before kick-off and so rather than walk to the far end where there was no cover we sat with the home supporters. Town did not turn up and we got thumped 4-0, it was more than embarrassing and we left with five minutes to go. Needless to say our car was blocked in – not a night to remember.

In the summer of 1996, there was significant activity in the transfer market. The successful strike force of Andy Booth and Ronnie Jepson departed; Boothy to Wednesday for £2.7 million and Jeppo to Bury for a reported fee of £40,000. In came Andy Morrison, Marcus Stewart and Andy Payton, who with 17 was by far the leading scorer. The other major signings suffers with injuries and the transfer of Ronnie Jepson proved to be an error of judgement as there was no big forward to hold the ball and lead the line. Finishing in 20th place was a disappointment.

Town reached the third round of the Coca Cola Cup but were on the receiving end of a 5-1 drubbing at Middlesbrough in front of 5,000 travelling fans. I got a ticket for one of my work colleagues, David Thompson, who enjoyed the game even though he sat in the away end.

The quality of Juninho and Ravennelli was too much for a Town team lacking confidence.

CHAPTER 14

The Great Escape

In 1997/1998 Town equalled their worst start to a league campaign by not recording a win until the 15th game of the season. Brian Horton was dismissed and replaced by former player Peter Jackson who made some shrewd signings in Lee Richardson, Barry Horne and Wayne 'The Chief' Allison who cost a large fee.

One of the highlights of the season was the 1-0 win at Maine Road over Manchester City. The match was played on a Friday evening and was televised. This was the second victory of the season and the first away from home. The goal by Rob Edwards was the culmination of a move involving sixteen passes.

Marcus Stewart was the leading goal scorer in the league with 15 goals followed by Paul Dalton with 13.No doubt some of these came from 'assists' from big Wayne who contributed 6 from 27 appearances.

A run of 4 wins and 2 draws during March and April ensured safety after relegation had seemed inevitable. Possibly with the pressure off, the Town players relaxed during the final game of the season. Port Vale needed to win to avoid the drop and did so with an emphatic score line of 0-4 after the hard graft under manager Peter Jackson, it was disappointing finish. However nothing can alter the fact that this was indeed 'The Great Escape.'

CHAPTER 15
After the Great Escape

After a defeat in the opening game of the season at Bury – new goalkeeper Nico Vaesen was sent off 9 minutes into his debut – Town got 19 out of 24 points in the next eight matches taking them to the top of the league. This run ended at Bolton with a 3--0 thumping; a disappointing trip for the Waterhouse clan although we found a good pub which served not only excellent beer but also tasty sandwiches – even 'she who must be obeyed' was impressed.

A win over Bradford City in November was marred by an injury to Barry Horne who did not play again that season – he was not replaced and was sadly missed. Normally we go to Oakwell when Town are playing, but on this particular Friday night, we decided to watch the match which was featured on Sky TV. The first half could only be described by Victor Meldrew – we could not believe it either as Town went in at the interval losing 6-0. The final score was 7-1. A friend of mine from Barnsley was on holiday at the time, got a paper abroad and until he arrive home thought the score was 1-1. By the time he had told this story half a dozen times he finally tumbled to the fact that we were not interested. The term 'ad nauseum' springs to mind.

We took our grandson to the next match and we beat Palace 4-0. He was deciding which team to adopt and both his mum and I thought we had cracked it when he dropped a bombshell the next day. Of all the teams to pick it was that lot who play next to the M621. Jesus wept!!

Sandra is a very difficult person for whom to buy presents; I fall for her trick every time when she says, 'When I see something I'll buy it. This of course means she spends twice as much as I would have done. Our wedding anniversary is 19th December – every year – and so my problem can be merged with Christmas. In 1998 I made suggestion after suggestion and hint after hint but to no avail. This was very frustrating as I knew in the end it would cost me dear.

At the time, the editor of the Town programme would print from time to time, articles contributed by supporters and so I decided to air my views on what do you buy for a woman who has everything. I waffled on about holidays, jewellery, clothes (designer of course – something which has class and will not date), expensive perfumes and even thought about a new kitchen but that was going a bit too far.

Then I had a flash of inspiration. The next Town match was on the very day, 19th December. That was it. I would take her on a wonderful day out to Gresty Road, Crewe with no expense spared on a few drinks and then fish and chips out of the paper. I know how to treat a lady. The queue at the fish and chip shop was so long we went back to the car and ate the sandwiches we had brought ' just in case'. I did try – honest. Marcus Stewart popped in a couple of goals and we won 2-1

I got my masterpiece typed up and sent it to the Town office and it appeared in the programme for the Boxing Day match against Grimsby. Quite a few people came up to us and asked Sandra if she had seen the programme. She gave the usual response that she read the programme the next morning over breakfast, and indeed, she did not see it until then. I was waiting for the reaction of nuclear proportions when I saw her smile. 'Quite funny' she said. Fortunately Sandra has a sense of humour – at times. I didn't keep a copy of the article but a couple of years later had another piece in the programme in the Soapbox column.

A disappointing run in to the end of the season, with only one win (against Bradford City) in the last 11 games saw Town finish in 10th spot. In my view the injury to Barry Horne was the pivotal incident. Marcus Stewart was top scorer with 22 goals in 43 games.

Defeat away to Derby County in a 5th round replay meant Town had a reasonable FA Cup run while in the League Cup, after holding Everton to a 1-1 draw in the first leg, the Toffees scraped a 2-1 win at Goodison Park to win the tie on aggregate. Off the field the long running saga of a takeover by multi-millionaire Barry Rubery was determined in January but the effect of this was to be felt after the season ended.

In a blaze of publicity Steve Bruce was appointed manager following the surprise dismissal of Peter Jackson. Several signings were made with the most spectacular being the acquisition of George Donnis from AEK Athens.

He was to make only 10 starts and a further 10 appearances from the bench; what a waste of money. No wonder he soon became known as 'kebab'.

Steve Bruce won over many supporters and following a run of six wins in October/November, Town sat proudly at the top of the table. But for what I can only think were financial reasons, leading scorer Marcus Stewart was sold to promotion rivals Ipswich Town and promptly got the winning goal on his debut when the two sides met. (As the ink was still drying on the transfer forms.) The sale was to have far reaching repercussions next season. Town lost the last two games of the season and the chance of a play off place.

We had travelled to several away games, particularly in the first half of the season. When parking my car at a garage near to Oakwell, I commented to the man who was taking the money that it was a waste of time coming here as we always lost – which we did 4-2 despite the fact that we were having a good run. A trip to Maine Road brought the now customary 1-0 win thanks to Chris Beech – how times change!!.

The televised 3rd round FA Cup tie against Liverpool attracted the largest gate at the new stadium but after Town missed a couple of good chances, the visitors scored twice and showed a bit of extra class with a 2-0 win. In the Worthington Cup, a tremendous strike by Kenny Irons sank Chelsea at Stamford Bridge in round 3 but Town went down 2-1 to a strong Wimbledon side at home in the next round.

CHAPTER 16

The Start of the Slippery Slope

The emphatic manner in which Town were beaten in the final two games of the previous season did not augur well for 2000/2001; however after a 2-1 defeat at home against an average Watford team, there was jubilation with a 3-2 win at Hillsborough Particularly as Wednesday had only just dropped out of the Premier League. Any celebrations were short lived as the next victory did not come until 2nd December. Steve Bruce was dismissed in October leaving Lou Macari to pick up the pieces. Incredibly Lou won the manager of the month award for December with an unbeaten run of seven games with five wins and two draws. The loan signing of Peter Ndlovu was a masterstroke. The Zimbabwean scored 4 goals in 6 matches but following his return to Birmingham City, Town went another seven games without a win.

The return of the talismanic Andy Booth in March brought hope when he scored on his second 'debut' in a 4-1 thrashing of Portsmouth. However on the last day of the season, Town were still in danger of relegation although that would mean Town losing and Crystal Palace winning away at Stockport. The optimists said Town could hold high flying Birmingham at home and so there was no real problem but the pessimists, myself included, thought the Blues would want to go into the play offs with confidence and would be 'up for it'; Palace's away record was not too bad and Stockport were in lower mid table with nothing to play for.

Currently there is a radio programme which asks football supporters to ring or text with instances of a five minute period they would wish to be struck from the records. I was tempted to ring in but bottled it. With 5 minutes to go on that fateful day 6th May 2001, Town were safe. Then there was a moment of madness from goalkeeper Nico Vaesen. Boa Morte picked up a clearance on the right wing and ambled down the flank. There was little danger as he was a predominately a left footed player with his right leg a mere swinger, which meant he would have to stop and then cut inside. For some unknown reason, Nico came off his line even though two defenders were closing in. Boa Morte saw him and curled a left foot shot round the keeper with no other Birmingham player within 20 yards. The Cowshed groaned – we all did.

The score at Stockport in injury time was 0-0, there was still hope. A Stockport player was brought down on the Palace box, the players stopped but the referee waved play on. The Stockport defenders had gone up field to celebrate with their colleagues and when the Palace keeper kicked the ball downfield, the experienced Dougie Freedman was in splendid isolation. Needless to say, he scored. Palace had made their great escape and Town had thrown it away. What a way to go down. To make matters worse one of the girls in the office at work was at the game – a Birmingham supporter – and on the following Monday commented that she had not seen a side relegated before. She made the tea for the whole of that week; the rota was scrapped.

Lou Macari remained in charge but with finances tight as Barry Rubery wanted to sell the club, several of the high earners departed. The loan signing of teenager Leon Knight from Chelsea proved to be a brilliant move. He netted 16 goals from 31 appearances in the league. Andy Booth scored 11. Somehow Town qualified for the play offs but this time Brentford got their revenge with Town having to play without suspended Leon Knight.

The takeover was completed in January 2002 with Town fan David Taylor installed as chairman. The family trips out did not bring Town much success with defeat at an icily cold Tranmere and draws at Oldham, Bury and Wigan. There was some success in the LDV Vans Trophy when defeat to Blackpool meant Town had come within 180 minutes of a place in a showpiece final.

CHAPTER 17

Relegation – A Swift Return

In the close season, Lou Macari was dismissed despite halting the slide and almost getting promotion, and Mick Wadsworth was appointed in his place apparently on the recommendation of Sir Bobby Robson. With only five goals scored in the first eleven league games, the problem was obvious; in fact Town ended the season as the lowest scorers in the Division. Of the thirty nine goals scored Martin Smith got seventeen, on returning to the side after a long time out injured.

Town ended the season in 22nd position- five points from safety-- with one consolation; we did the double over Barnsley. In January, the financial plight became public and in March Mick Wadsworth paid the price for some dismal performances and was dismissed. Season 2002/2003 had not been one to remember.

In the summer Administrators were appointed and I lost the value of my shares. With others I had also helped the club by paying for future season tickets; whilst the new owner agreed to accepting one year, I could have been left high and dry for the other 2 years. Fortunately I had paid by credit card and persuaded the card company to cough up as the service of providing football matches had not been made as promised

The new owner, Ken Davy deserves the thanks of all Town supporters as without him we could have been faced with the situation now being suffered by Halifax Town who I am pleased to say at the time of writing are doing well in the Unibond League – hopefully they can climb back up the pyramid quickly.

Peter Jackson was appointed as manager in June and set about finding players to form a team in time for the kick off in August. Predictably, the season got off to a poor start and it was not until the fifth game that a win was recorded. One of the early defeats was at home against York City. I was umpiring a match at Studley Royal in the York Senior Cricket League; while most of the players had leanings towards City, one of the Studley Royal batsmen was a Town fan. We took a bit of stick both during and after the match which, in my opinion, justified turning down a strong appeal for LBW when he was at the crease.

After scoring 16 goals in 26 league appearances Jon Stead was transferred to Blackburn Rovers for a large fee and although Town would miss his goals it was a good move. Jon achieved an ambition to play at the top level and no doubt the money came in handy. Pawel Abbott was signed from Preston as a replacement and in twelve appearances scored 5 goals.

There were mixed fortunes in the cup competitions. A televised first round defeat in the FA Cup at non league Accrington Stanley was a disaster. Jon Worthington was dismissed early on for an alleged foul tackle but Town held out magnificently until the last minute when an Accrington sub who had definitely eaten all the pies scored a once in a lifetime goal which brought a stunned silence in our household. Another instance for Victor Meldrew – we could not believe it either. Even the BBC pundits were sympathetic towards Town.

Derby County were beaten 2-1 in the first round at home in the Carling Cup. The next round took Town to Sunderland. Once again Sandra and I took our preparations very seriously; a brisk walk on the seafront was followed by coffee and bacon sandwiches. What else does one do? It paid off as Town hammered the Black Cats 4-2. The cup run ended in a 1-0 defeat at Reading.

On 25th January Town travelled to York City, which for us, was really a home fixture. Nic May, the son of one of our neighbours was the York mascot and he was a little surprised when the chant of 'There's only Nicky May ' rang out loud and clear from the away end as he left the field prior to kick off. My thanks to the Town supporters who joined in. The teams were more or less level in the league table and the result looked like ending up a 0-0 draw when Town broke away. The York keeper could only parry the ball and Danny Schofield obliged. Two minutes to go and it got better. Latching on to a through ball sub David Mirfin took it in his stride, drew the keeper to score a goal of which Alan Shearer would have been proud. For a centre back it was a magnificent effort. After that Town prospered and City had a torrid time and finished up bottom of the Division to be relegated to the Conference.

With three matches to go, Town needed three points to secure an automatic promotion place. A draw at Hull, who were to finish as runners up to Doncaster, was deemed to be satisfactory and a huge crowd of over 18,000 assembled at the McAlpine to witness promotion with a victory over Mansfield. They were to be disappointed as the Stags outplayed Town and won 3-1.

Still, a win at mid table Cheltenham would do the trick and with Town leading 1-0 well into the second half everything in the garden was rosy; then Pav Abbott, intent on keeping possession, telegraphed a back pass to the keeper which was intercepted by a Cheltenham forward who equalised. The term 'telegraphed ' may be lost on most on the younger readers but I suppose we can say it was a way of communicating before the advent of text messages. Town could not force a winner and with Torquay getting an excellent (for them not Town) away win, we were pipped at the post on goal difference.

CHAPTER 18

Glory in the Play Offs

The first leg of the semi final was played at Sincil Bank, the home of Lincoln City. I was committed to umpiring at cricket and so Sandra and Jane went to the McAlpine to watch the game on a big screen. Goals from Iffy Onuora, brought in by Peter Jackson to bolster the attack, and Dave Mirfin gave Town a 2-1 advantage for the second leg at home. Surely there would not be any more slip ups but Town had a habit of doing things the hard way and when Lincoln went 2-0 up to put them ahead on aggregate, the pessimists were airing their views. Danny Schofield pulled a goal back from the penalty spot and with extra time looming Rob Edwards wrote his name into the history books. His goal at Maine Road over which I eulogised earlier paled into insignificance when in the 83rd minute he found himself unmarked in the Lincoln box with the ball on his right foot – not his stronger. However with aplomb he put the ball into the corner of the goal to put Town ahead on aggregate. The last seven minutes were nerve-wracking but the relief at the final whistle was apparent on three sides of the stadium.

The final, at Cardiff, was scheduled for the Bank Holiday week end at the end of May and which fool had booked a holiday in Canada.? I can only plead 'Guilty, me lud' It was left to the females to represent the Waterhouse clan at the Millennium Stadium with Karen and Jane taking Karen's twin daughters Claire and Lexie..The result was the icing on the cake; the journey down went smoothly and the parking arrangements were excellent as were the facilities at the stadium.

The match? Town's opponents were Mansfield who had outplayed the Terriers in the penultimate league match game and on this basis were installed as favourites by the pundits on TV. After ninety minutes there were no goals although there was a scare late on when Mansfield got the ball in the Town net only for an alert linesman to signal that before the ball was crossed it had gone over the dead ball line. Panic over. Extra time prolonged the stalemate and the girls had to endure a penalty shoot out.

The preparations by Peter Jackson now paid off. Apparently when practising penalties Peter replicated the situation which could, and, of course, did arise. Penalty takers had to walk from the centre circle and wait while 'opponents' did the same. The tension, albeit without a crowd, was created and this stood Town in good stead. All the four players who were required were successful whilst the Mansfield players appeared to be mentally unprepared and scored only once. Town had not only won the cup but had secured promotion. A picture of Claire and Lexie with the trophy takes pride of place in our dining room. Apparently on the journey back north, a couple of Mansfield supporters were mooning as the car overtook their coach; the two eleven year old girls thought this was hilarious.

But what of Sandra and myself who had 'absented ourselves'. We had met up with my nephew Roger who lived in Calgary – he motored up to Banff and we took him out for a few drinks and a meal. His sporting allegiance had temporarily moved from the team that plays near the M621 to Calgary Flames who had, against the odds, qualified for the equivalent of our play-offs in the North American ice hockey league. In a seven match series they

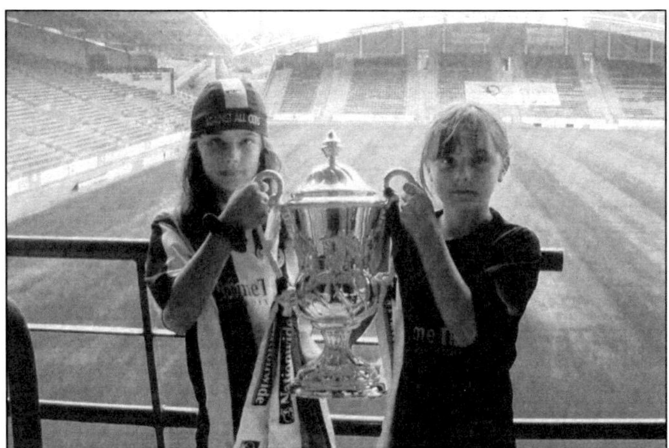

Claire and Lexie Rhodes (grandaughters) with the Play Off Trophy for League Two. The snapper was Ann Hough (Director and Secretary HTAFC)

lost out but won the game we saw. He stayed in our room at the hotel and I bought his breakfast. He could not then refuse my request for him to leave a message at our hotel with the result of the match at Cardiff – we were touring around and did not have internet access.

The red button was flashing as we got to our room and it was with some trepidation that I took the message. 'Don't shoot the messenger' it began and then after a chuckle continued 'But you got through'. We celebrated by going out for some fish and chips at a small cafe owned by a couple from Blackburn. The quality was very good but I suppose Lancashire fish and chips do rank second to those from God's own county. One of the first jobs on our return was to buy the video.

CHAPTER 19

Consolidation in League One

Off the pitch it was a case of all change. The Football League re-branded its structure; Division 1 became the Championship, Division 2 was re-named League 1 and Division 3 League 2. Closer to home the ten- year sponsorship by Alfred McAlpine expired and in stepped former Town chairman Graham Leslie through his company Galpharm which became the new name for the stadium. It was now a case of 'Down at the Pharm'.

Season 2004/2005 started well with a 3-2 away win over Stockport with goals by Tony Carss, Andy Booth and Pawel Abbott.Andy again got into double figures with ten goals in 25 appearances but it was Pawel who was by far the leading scorer with 26 goals from 36 starts and 8 from the bench. In September he scored his first senior hat trick in the 3-0 victory against Port Vale. We normally go to Vale Park but I had a cricket umpiring commitment; it was the final game of the cricket season and my appointment involved a match on which the championship depended and so was not one to miss. That would have been the only away match I would have seen Town win as our visits to Blackpool, Barnsley, Bradford, Hull and Tranmere produced only one point.

Sandra and I went to China on holiday in March with Town too near the relegation zone for comfort; there was no way we could get the results as we toured round what is a fascinating country. The flight home landed at Heathrow in the evening and we arranged to stay in a hotel and continue our journey home the next day. Even before going to the bar for a drink, like a true supporter I switched on the TV to discover that Town had won all three games while we were away. That was the start of a tremendous finale to the season; in the last 9 matches out of 27 points available Town got 25 dropping only the two points at home to Colchester United in a 2-2 draw. From flirting with relegation Town only missed the play- offs by one point.

During the close season, Peter Jackson brought in Mark Hudson, Martin McIntosh and Gary Taylor-Fletcher (GTF) and it was the latter who was to have the greatest impact. In the league Town were always there and there abouts until the end of the season. The drama came in the major cup competitions after a lean time in recent years. In the Carling Cup a stunning 4-2 win at Chesterfield in round 1 gave Town an attractive tie at Blackburn; this was very convenient for Sandra and me as Karen lives in Waterfoot and at the time was working in Blackburn. We got the tickets and invited ourselves to tea with Karen agreeing to act as chauffeur. Virtually every car on the way to the match was sporting blue and white colours and we thought that most of them would be carrying supporters for the home team. Not so – of the attendance of just under 12,000 at least half were from Huddersfield. One of my friends was stuck in traffic and missed the first 30 minutes.

With Town 2-0 down in the second half, the away support turned up the volume and Pav Abbott obliged with a goal.The Premier League outfit were hanging on but then Craig Bellamy (love him or hate him but he has class) broke away to make the score 3-1. Town were not disgraced and received a tremendous ovation from the travelling faithful at the end of a very entertaining game despite the result.

That was the starter; the main course was to come in the FA Cup. Town were in the 3rd round draw after beating two non-league sides in Welling and Worcester. When Chelsea came out of the hat, I said to Sandra 'We could do with them' and so, as it says in the Bible, it came to pass. By the end of the day the Waterhouse clan had sorted out the arrangements – all we needed were the tickets. Karen was going to stay with her sister-in-law at Leighton Buzzard while Sandra and I decided to go by train. We got a cheap fare for going down on the Saturday but could not get one for the return journey and so treated ourselves by staying at a posh hotel near Piccadilly – fortunately they had an offer on.

We met up with the others, Karen, Jane, Lexie and Claire inside the ground. Whilst we had made do with a sandwich they had lunched at a bistro on the Kings Road. We thought that if we could keep Chelsea out for 20 minutes we might have a chance but when Carlton Cole headed the ball home after a lucky rebound we realised we had a lot on our plate – in fact, the first half hour was played inside the Town half. The storm was weathered and with eleven minutes to go it was still only 1-0 to the aristocrats of the Premier

League. Then Tom Clarke broke up a Chelsea attack and passed the ball to Michael Collins on the right wing. Michael threaded a through ball and GTF (Gran Turismo Forward!!) outpaced the Chelsea defence to place the ball in the corner of the goal a mere 20 yards from where we were sitting we were not seated for long. Town pressed forward and Mourinho sent on two of his big guns; one of them, the Dutch international Robben, got past Dave Mirfin and crossed the ball for the Icelander Gudjohnsen to prod home the winner. The ovation at Blackburn was nothing to compare with that at Stamford Bridge as 7,000 Town fans cheered for a full twenty minutes after the game had ended. Although our team had lost, we were proud supporters as we had steak and chips at an Angus Steak Bar in Piccadilly Circus.

In the league Town were handily placed for an automatic promotion spot with five games to go but of the last fifteen points available, we got only five and ended up in fourth position which meant a play-off semi-final against Barnsley. The optimists pointed out that we had drawn at Oakwell and won at the Galpharm but the pessimists looked at Town's poor form in the last five games of the regular season. I thought we were a bit fortunate to win 1-0 in the first leg but who cares in the play-offs. At the Galpharm, the Tykes went one up but Jon Worthington restored Town's aggregate lead; however in the second half Barnsley played well and although the winning goals came late on, unfortunately, I have to say, that over the two legs they just about deserved to go through to the final where they beat Swansea. This was a disappointing end to a season which had promised much.

There was one minor success story during the season off the field. Our usual pilgrimage to Vale Park on March 25th 2006 produced a little gem of an eating place. Walking down the road with the ground on the right and looking for somewhere to eat and drink, we spotted the Strawberry Cafe which, from the outside was not very pretentious, but it had caught the imagination of the two girls and so we went in.

Half the menu was for Caribbean dishes but I looked on the next table and saw a man having a large jacket potato with a cheese filling; that was good enough for Karen and Claire but I preferred chilli con carne rather than cheese. Three of us catered for. Lexie likes sausage sandwiches and opted for the jumbo variety. We ordered three cokes and a coffee and had not long to wait before our lunch arrived.

The jacket potatoes came first and they were immense but when the sausage sandwich was produced we were staggered – extra large jumbo would have been a better description. Little Lexie, whose appetite can vary between a sparrow and an elephant, got stuck in and managed to clear her plate; the sparrows had obviously flown away.

I realised that I had not looked at the menu and had no idea what the bill may come to; there was a pleasant surprise to come as the food and drinks added up to just over £10 – magnificent value. It was agreed there and then that next season the visit to Port Vale would include lunch at the Strawberry. It was not to be.

Sandra and I decided to organise a family holiday during the half term holiday in October 2007 and with one of our investments doing particularly well booked a five day break in New York. This was done before the football fixtures were published. Sod's Law came into play. On the Saturday we flew to the Big Apple there was no prize for guessing where Town were playing – just as with the play off final I had double booked. After checking in following a hair raising ride in a yellow cab from Kennedy Airport to Manhattan we set off out for a meal. With the time difference the soccer results would be on the internet and a very efficient gentleman of German extraction who was at the Front Desk printed out the scores for all divisions- Port Vale 1 Huddersfield Town 2. We would have celebrated by having strawberries and cream for pudding but portions in the States are so large, we had to give that idea a miss.

Mrs K Rhodes (Elder daughter) with daughters Lexi and Claire

CHAPTER 20

The Anti Climax

After the excitement of the previous season when the average home game was over 13,000, season 2006/2007 was, to say the least, a disappointment. Instead of visiting clubs in the Premier League, Town lost in the first round of each cup competition. This was particularly galling as each defeat was at home.

In the league, a 5-1 defeat at Nottingham Forest was too much for the Board of Directors and three days later Peter Jackson was dismissed on 6th March. On 11th April Andy Ritchie was appointed. Town finished in 15th place mainly due to drawing seventeen games.

The highlights of the season indicate the lack of success. On 8th August Gary Taylor – Fletcher scored a goal with a spectacular volley with the outside of his right foot at the Panasonic end against Rotherham. This proved to be the 500,000th league goal and later GTF received an award in recognition of this feat. It was at this end that Iain Dunn scored the first Golden Goal. I am sure someone could make up a quiz question out of those incidents.

One other notable feat belonged to Matt Glennon who became the first Town goalkeeper to save three penalties in one match. He did this against Crewe Alexandra on 24th February at the South Stand end – Town lost the match 2-1.

One bright spot in an unforgettable season was the fact that Town supporters went away for the summer cherishing a victory in the last match of the season at the Galpharm. This may not mean much to those who did not witness the debacles against Portsmouth, Port Vale and Birmingham, but for me it did ease the pain. The average league attendance of 10,569- a decrease of almost 2,500 from the previous season – reflected the feeling of Town supporters.

Season 2007/2008 started well with a 2-0 home win over Yeovil but Town were inconsistent and throughout the campaign remained in mid to lower mid-table. Early exits from the Carling Cup and the Johnstone Paint Trophy – the latter a 4-1 thumping at Grimsby brought fears of another cup whitewash. In the FA Cup first round the score at Accrington at half time was 0-2 and memories of that humiliating defeat on television four years previously loomed large. The second half was a different story and Town won 3-2 with goals from Malvin Kamara (2) and Luke Beckett. Grimsby came to the Galpharm in round 2 and Town exacted revenge for the JP Trophy defeat by beating the Mariners 3-0..The third round and in the draw with the big boys; Birmingham City, struggling in the Premier League were Town's opponents and in front of a crowd of 13,410 were dumped out of the cup as Town won 2-1.

Round 4 saw Town drawn away at Oldham; a difficult match and a local derby. We found not only a new parking spot but also a new hostelry which sold an excellent pint of bitter. The Waterhouse clan had got their preparations right and so now it was up to the team. After Luke Beckett had scored at the far end, Town held on for a hard fought 1-0 win.

Bring on Man U was the cry; however we were not to be disappointed as we drew Chelsea away again – chance to get revenge for that narrow defeat two years previously. Within hours Karen had made the arrangements; the Waterhouse/Rhodes (her married name) family were booked in with her sister -in-law, Barbara, who lives at Leighton Buzzard, to stay Friday and Saturday nights. We assembled at the Rhodes residence at Waterfoot on Friday morning and travelled to Leighton Buzzard. On the Saturday morning we went for a walk with Barbara, her husband Daniel and their labrador, Grace, before setting off to the match.

We got off the tube at Earl's Court and looked for a suitable place for something to eat and drink. I failed miserably; we ended up buying a sandwich from a Tesco store near the ground and having our alfresco lunch sitting on a bench in Brompton Cemetery.Our seats were better than last time and unfortunately had a good view of Frank Lampard opening the scoring for the Blues; we were not sitting when Michael Collins latched on to a through ball from James Berrett and beat the Chelsea keeper to equalise right on the stroke of half-time.

The second half started well with Town attacking 'our' end – 7,000 fans surely making an extra man. Against the run of play, Chelsea broke away twice to win 3-1 but what a match! On the tube back to Euston we chatted to some Chelsea fans who said it was the best game of the season at Stamford Bridge; possibly it was because the prices had virtually been halved and they had won!!.

We went to Daniel's local pub for a meal in the evening; the food was very good in marked contrast to the service, which prompted the landlord to provide a cheese board free. It was then back to Barbara and Daniel's for coffee and liqueurs before watching Match of the Day – we lost again!! Sandra and I arrived home during Sunday afternoon absolutely exhausted, but what a fabulous weekend.

League form continued to be mixed and in April our manager, Andy Ritchie, departed with Gerry Murphy coming in as caretaker. Form improved and Town rose up the table to finish in tenth place; the highlight of Gerry's reign was the victory over Leeds thanks to a header from Andy Holdsworth at the Panansonic stand end in the second half.

Stan Ternent and Ronnie Jepson were appointed just before the end of the season but left Gerry in charge for the last match. Apart from the cup run it had been another disappointing campaign and more than one season -ticket holder commented that they may not renew next time.

CHAPTER 21

The Centenary Year

Stan Ternent made his mark early on in the close season by signing several new players and, with Dave Mirfin the only notable departure had a huge squad of players for the prestigious match against Arsenal for the Herbert Chapman Trophy. Arsenal were competing in a tournament abroad and played their second team in the first half against the Town first team. In the second half, it was Arsenal third team against Town second team, all of whom had recent experience in first team football either at the Galpharm or with their previous clubs. For the record Arsenal won 2-1.

Expectations were high and the 1-1 draw in the opening match against Stockport County, newly promoted after winning the League 2 play off final, was seen as a disappointing start. We missed that match and the 4-0 victory over Bradford City in the Carling Cup in mid-week as we were away in Seahouses on the annual family holiday. The rented house coped with 4 adults, 3 teenagers and 2 labradors and a good time was had by all, particularly the dogs who didn't seem to notice that the sea was cold.

The next home match was against another promoted side, MK Dons, who outplayed us and deserved their 3-1 win. After losing the next game at Millwall we were bottom of the league with 2 points from 5 games. This was not what we had expected. However the situation improved slightly – it couldn't have got any worse – and at the end of September we had sufficient faith to make the usual pilgrimage to Oldham who were playing well at the time. Our pre-match preparations went well; car parking was easy and the bitter in excellent form at the pub we had discovered the previous season. When Ian Craney put us ahead we had high hopes but Oldham equalised and the game was drawn. The effort from the Town players could not be faulted and we enjoyed our day out.

Normally we would go to Hartlepool but mid-week at the end of October did not catch the imagination and so we listened to Radio Leeds with Paul Ogden and Kieran O'Regan, who could not hide their disappointment when Town let in 3 late goals which turned a possible 3-2 victory into a demoralising 5-3 defeat. The following Saturday it got worse with a 4-0 thumping at Peterborough. The final straw came on 8th November when Port Vale, struggling in League 2 scored 3 late goals to win 4-3. If ever defeat was snatched from the jaws of victory this was it.

A position of 16th in the league and out of all the cup competitions was clearly not good enough following the investment in players and Stan Ternent, Ronnie Jepson and the rest of the management team departed. Caretaker managers Gerry Murphy and Graham Mitchell took over for the short trip to Elland Road. Although the ground is nearer than the Galpharm, we never go there because I object to being locked in after the match. I would park my car in Beeston, a 10/15 minute walk away but there are no police in the area 45 minutes after the final whistle. Radio Leeds brought us commentary of that late late winner from Michael Collins and this was the signal for the opening of a good bottle of red wine at Waterhouse Towers.

The next away trip was to Carlisle on Boxing Day. The journey up the M6 was OK the company and quality of beer at Carlisle rugby club was superb. Once we had cleared the traffic and reached the motorway, the journey back went well. What a pity about the 'entertainment' between 3pm and 4.50pm. A 3-0 defeat which was humiliating. The newly appointed manager, Lee Clark, would no doubt have had some harsh words to say after that shambles.

By the middle of January Town were in eighth place in the league and had high hopes of getting a result at league leaders Leicester City. Karen, Sandra and I decided the team would need some support and we set off in good spirits. After parking the car at Leicester rugby club, we had a look round the city centre, found an excellent pint at the Market Tavern followed by a good lunch at Bella Italia(we had a coupon offering two meals for the price of one) We had got our preparations right. 'Come on lads', we thought, 'its up to you now'. Phil Jevons put us ahead but we had hardly got into the swing of 'Top of the league, you're having a laugh' when the Foxes equalised. Still we would have settled for 1-1 at half time. Again we went ahead when Keigan Parker scored a superb goal but the home side soon equalised and then added two more to win 4-2.After negotiating the one way system in Leicester we arrived home having had a good day out. A pity about the result, but at least Town had contributed to a tremendous game.

The next and last outing of the season was the short trip to Stockport; I have not seen a worse pitch in the league in all the years I have been following Town. It was a good job the tide was out. Michael Collins put us ahead and that was the way it stayed until deep in to time added on when their right winger got away; I thought he was offside. His fierce cross was beaten out by Alex Smithies but tragedy struck when the ball hit Nathan Clarke in the face and rebounded into the net. Two points had been lost. Town were in 10th position and with 13 games to play, a good run could lead to a play -off place.

Unfortunately a run of 7 games without a win meant Town finished in 9th place, eight points adrift of the last play off place, even though four of the last five away matches were won with the other being drawn.

Andy Booth, a living legend, missed most of the season because of injury and announced his retirement but not before he had scored six goals in the last four matches. He will be missed but hopefully Lee Clark will find a replacement as, in my opinion, a big centre forward who can lead the line and score goals is a vital part of any successful team.

The Centenary season was eventful if not as successful as we had hoped, apart from doing the double over the lads from LS11. However confidence is high and Sandra and I have upgraded our season tickets to join the White Rose Club which means we will have a posh seat and the facility to enjoy a drink in pleasant surroundings before and after the game. I think Town will do well – but have I heard that before?

CHAPTER 22

Huddersfield Town Video Team

In May 1987, I was invited to join the video team for the following season as a commentator. I was to share the duties with my friend John Morgan who wanted to continue with the video team but also to carry on with his radio work doing hospital broadcasts. At the time, matches in the lower divisions were not covered automatically by the TV companies and, apart from the odd goal flash on a local TV news programme, the only way of seeing pictures of Town games was via the club video. Nowadays the programme 'Goals on Sunday' includes all divisions and the coverage on Look North and Calendar is better.

John worked out a rota and my debut was to be August 25th when Town were scheduled to play Rotherham United in the second leg of a first round tie in the Littlewoods Challenge Cup. During the summer I had borrowed some videos from the previous season to get an idea as to what was involved, but as further preparation, went to Millmoor to see the first leg; I treated myself to a seat in the main stand and throughout the game did a mental commentary.

I had already met Nigel Schofield, the man in charge, his wife Jayne, who keyed in the team details and Wilf Charlton who assisted Nigel and usually was in charge of the camera for the first half with Nigel taking over after the interval. After a hectic car journey from York to Leeds Road on a bright Tuesday evening we arrived about 35 minutes before kick-off and I had a quick look at the programme, mainly to see who was playing for Rotherham and to pick up any other trivia I could introduce to the commentary at the appropriate time.

The plan was for me to record an introduction to the game and to go through the teams; this would be done 15 minutes before the players came on to the field and suited me as any error could be corrected. At a quarter past seven we were all set when disaster struck; the power supply went off. Brian Leeming, maintenance electrician, was summoned and I was told to keep out of the way. After much ado, power was restored as the players appeared on the field. Plan B would have been handy but there was no Plan B and so I just carried on as I thought was best.

No one made any adverse comments after the match and so I considered my performance to be OK. Out of curiosity and particularly in view of the unusual circumstances, I borrowed a tape of the game to watch at home. During the journey back to York, Sandra who had watched from her usual seat in the stand, commented that Daryl Pugh had played quite well to which my reply was ' He wasn't playing'. The frosty response was 'Oh, you ignored the team changes then'. Throughout the match I had called the Rotherham number eleven 'Harrison' and he had been quite prominent. So what you might say. OK there was a mistake. However which was one of Daryl's former clubs ? Yes, Huddersfield Town- not then, the best of starts.

In contrast to the hectic activity of that Tuesday evening, the match on the following Saturday at home to Shrewsbury could be classed as boring. There were no problems with the power supply or team changes; in fact, I got a copy of the official team sheet. The result was a 0-0l draw with Town unable to break down a stubborn defence well marshalled by Nigel Pearson, who later went on to play at a higher level with Sheffield Wednesday and Middlesbrough.

All the Town home games were covered and, in addition to the sales in the club shop, I understand the manager(s) used them. Eoin Hand once told me how much he enjoyed the videos, particularly when the sound was turned down; no doubt an example of his Irish sense of humour. Apparently, another manager when using the tape as evidence in appealing against a Town player having been sent off, had the commentary deleted as my version of events did not coincide with his.

Sometimes the video team were allowed an 'away day'. The most popular trip was to Bury where the matches always had plenty of goals. In 1989 Town won 6-0 and after playing with a stiff breeze at their backs were only leading by a single goal with time running out in the first half. I commented that a second goal would ease the pressure for the second period when up popped Craig Maskell right on cue. As the players came off the pitch I said 'That goal could be vital for Town who will have problems against the wind after the break'. The commentator's curse came into effect as Town adapted to the conditions and scored four more goals in a very one-sided second half.

In the following year Bury exacted revenge with the score line being reversed. Town were well and truly interred on the day. In 1991 Town were 4-0 down after 35 minutes and I feared the worst but Iwan Roberts pulled one back before half time. I ventured to comment somewhat optimistically, that the Terriers were still in the game; they certainly were when Phil Starbuck scored twice and when big Iwan nodded in the equaliser from Simon Ireland's cross, the recovery was complete. I remember saying it was the best comeback since Lazarus.

The feature of a visit to the Hawthorns was the look on Nigel Schofield's face when he saw a lady in the executive box next to our camera position devouring a massive helping of chilli con carne and rice. Nigel had forgotten his sandwiches and the bar at West Bromwich only sold crisps. However at Mansfield it was my turn to be embarrassed; the monitor was placed just in front of me on the roof of the gents toilet block but when I averted my eyes I saw a lady emerging, fully dressed I might add, from the ladies. Yes, I had a perfect view of the door to the female facilities and got some funny looks during the match.

I am not very good with heights and to get into the gantry at Burnden Park, Bolton it was necessary to climb on to the roof of the main stand, walk about five yards on a plank with a dodgy hand- rail and then drop down a ladder. Just as I was walking the plank, Sandra and Jane emerged from a sweet shop across the road and had to do a double take. Yes, it really was me clutching my clip board and hanging on for grim death. When Nigel said he fancied a cup of tea my response was in the negative, I was not risking life and limb. There was no toilet break at half time

The longest trips were to Gillingham and Swansea; the visit to the Vetch Field, next to the prison in Swansea was rewarded by Iwan Roberts scoring the only goal of the game to equal Craig Maskell's record of goals in all competitions set three seasons before. He broke the record in the last match of the season against Torquay, fittingly at Leeds Road. However the long journey to Gillingham was fruitless as after about five minutes play there was a power failure on our side of the ground which was being re-developed. The story goes that when the police were stood down once the match had. started, they decided to brew some tea which proved to be too much for the temporary supply. It was a foggy day all over the country and the drive home was not the most convivial.

In the first round of the FA Cup in 1989 Town were drawn away at Hartlepool. Not only was permission to film granted, it was positively encouraged by the home club. The facilities for the video team were not good as while Nigel could get his camera and assorted equipment on to a specially constructed sort of platform, I had to sit on the back row of the seats in the stand. We adapted to our surroundings and I made friends with the people sitting around me. The intro was recorded as usual much to the amusement of the spectators who got the impression that it was like being on Match of the Day.

The players came on to the field at 14.55 and we started our coverage with me pointing out little bits of trivia to set the scene. I was somewhat worried when the teams went back to the dressing rooms and Nigel made an executive decision.He switched the camera off leaving me in mid sentence. The gentleman on the PA system announced that the kick-off was put back 15 minutes so that the Huddersfield supporters could get into the ground. There had been an accident on the A19 and five coaches carrying Town fans had only just arrived at Victoria Park. With only two turnstiles open for over 200 fans clearly there was a problem.

How is that for a quiz question. When was the kick -off delayed at Hartlepool because of crowd congestion ? The answer 18th November 1989.

Nigel switched the camera back on and we carried on as if nothing had happened. Mike Cecere was brought down twice in the penalty area and twice he got up to put the ball into the back of the net. Town won 2-0 and went into the draw for round two. Nigel had done an additional tape at the request of the chap who managed the Hartlepool club shop and when we handed it over he had a broad smile on his face which was odd as his team had lost. 'Never mind' he said 'Tonight I shall see 'Pool on my TV set at home for the first time'. There was a happy ending for us all.

Another regular port of call was Gay Meadow at Shrewsbury. That is not strictly correct as we filmed from the science laboratory in the Technical College which was situated behind one goal. From that vantage point there was a panoramic view of the pitch as the laboratory was on the third floor. On our first visit their video cameraman was impressed that we had a commentator and the following year asked whether he could take my dulcet tones on to his film. A suitable fee was agreed – two pints of bitter in the bar after the game – and he and Nigel fiddled with the various plugs and we were in business. Apparently it was a success but Shrewsbury were relegated that season and so there was no trip the following year.

As work on the new stadium was under way, no repair work was carried out at Leeds Road. This was noticed particularly in November 1993 when Town played Preston in round 2 of the Autoglass Trophy. It was bitterly cold and made worse by a strong breeze which caught my right shoulder as it blasted its way through a gap in the wall of the studio room cut into the roof of the stand. After 90 minutes it was 0-0, the same after extra time and so on to penalties. There was no TV screen with pretty diagrams to provide an instant update of who had scored or missed; I had to keep a note of events with pen and paper and frozen fingers. Fortunately I got it right and Town were successful. From then on the studio was called 'Ice Station Zebra' after the well known film. That evening was without doubt the coldest I have ever felt at a football match.

Prior to home games we would congregate in the Greenall Suite where I would browse through the programme; one piece of information I could not get until then was the names of the officials who sometimes were sitting nearby having a cup of tea. One evening I checked that there were no changes when the referee Trevor West called Nigel over and asked if he could avoid showing his bald patch which tended to shine out like a beacon under floodlights – he tried to explain that it was not a bald patch at all but a solar panel to generate brain power. He had a good game as well as a sense of humour.

After home games we would go back to the Greenall Suite for the odd drink to let the traffic subside.. In 1993 we drew Arsenal in the second round of the Coca Cola Cup and when I approached the bar, my way was blocked by Steve Bould and Tony Adams; at 5 fee9 I am of moderate height but they towered over me – no wonder they won a lot of ball in the air. When they moved it was if someone had switched on the lights.

April 30th 1994 saw the final first team match at Leeds Road with Blackpool the visitors; I had not been told of any special arrangements and did my preparation as usual. On arriving at the ground I saw John Helm of Yorkshire Television and was told that he would be doing the commentary. John realised what had happened, looked at my clipboard and suggested we sit down and go through my notes. John has a vast knowledge of the game and I was quite chuffed when he picked out a couple of items which he had missed; they were only minor points and I am sure he included them as he could see how disappointed I was at not doing the commentary.

At half time I noticed a small crowd of people standing on Dalton Bank getting a free if not very good view of the pitch and said to John that my father had told me that when Town played Arsenal in 1932 in front of 67,037 spectators, those who could not see what was happening, left the ground and stood on Dalton Bank. As the players came out for the second half John got the cameraman to cover the small group standing on the bank and included comments on the information I had given giving me the thumbs up sign. That was the second time that afternoon I was chuffed.

The 1994/1995 season saw Town in the brand new McAlpine Stadium. Frantic efforts were made in the days leading up to the match against Wycombe

Wanderers to get the final bits and pieces in to place and the arrangements for the video team were understandably chaotic. I was commentating from the executive box at the end of the main stand towards what is now the Panasonic end of the ground. Not only did the box have tinted windows but its location was far from ideal. I understood that things were to get better and after doing two matches got a call from Club Secretary, Alan Sykes, asking me to arrive a bit earlier for the game on the forthcoming Saturday and to call in the office.

When I arrived I was introduced to Dave Jones (ex Radio Lancashire) who was to take over the commentary duties; my role was to provide the local information for Dave who lived in Blackburn and did not have the knowledge of Town matches in previous seasons. I did this for a couple of games but my heart was not in it and, having told Dave first out of courtesy, had a word with Alan Sykes who arranged for me to sit near the PA box (manned by Robert Tracey) in case I was needed. I got on well with Dave and we met up for a drink several times during the season.

I was called upon to do a commentary when England schoolboys played their Irish counterparts; Michael Owen and Nicky Butt were on the team sheet but there were so many substitutions.

My memories of the game are vague.

That rather low key match brought an end to my career as the 'John Motson' of Huddersfield Town – an experience which brought me a great deal of pleasure.

CHAPTER 23

Huddersfield Town Gentlemens' Sporting Club

In order to bring in some extra income and to make more use of the rooms used on match days as the President's Club and the Greenall Suite, the club secretary, George Binns came up with the concept of regular meetings involving sporting speakers. George convinced Ian Challenger, John Kaye and Jack Farrar that it was their idea and they assisted in drumming up support but, of course, George retained control over the purse strings. In February 1982, Peter Parfitt, the former Middlesex and England cricketer was the first speaker; he told us stories of his playing career and then we had an interval when David Armitage provided a sumptuous buffet supper. When we had all done justice to the pork pies, ham rolls and other similar delicacies, Peter answered questions on cricket in general and included some amusing anecdotes. Dennis Compton, the legendary batsman, noted for his racy lifestyle which, no doubt, influenced the manufacturers of Brylcream to pay Dennis to advertise their product, featured prominently. The story I remember concerned Dennis arriving late for a county match for Middlesex at Lords and finding that his team was batting decided to catch up on his sleep and was soon snoring away in a corner of the dressing room. It was young Parfitt's job to wake him when he was required. Peter did this but Dennis was unable to find his bat, probably the most important part of a batsman's equipment, and so he picked up the nearest 'piece of timber'.He went on to hit a flawless century.

The evening was a huge success and a list of speakers for the future was compiled. Ian Challenger, who was the first chairman, was well pleased as he was the area representative for the brewers Greenalls. A few months later, Neil Midgley the former referee with a good reputation as a speaker told us that he was going to arrive early and so he popped into a pub on the way to Huddersfield; however he made sure they sold Greenalls as he didn't wish to arrive smelling of beer. Ian's face was a picture but he did see the funny side – eventually.

The Sporting Club was an ideal starting point for potential speakers on the after-dinner circuit.Denis Law agreed to come following some arm twisting by George Binns but only on the basis that he answered questions rather than deliver from a prepared script At the end of the evening, Denis realised that all he had to do was to string together the stories he had told in his lengthy answers and he was on his way to being an entertaining and well paid performer; the latter point being very appealing to an Aberdonian. When asked about Town's famous 5-1 victory in an FA Cup replay at West Ham, he commented that the manager was Bill Shankly; at a suitable point I said Eddie Boot was the man in charge who had sent the players out in rubber-soled boots on an icy surface thereby giving Town a big advantage. Initially Denis was adamant and only conceded when George Binns went to the office to look at the official records..Despite that Denis enjoyed the evening particularly when chatting with his former team mates Brian Gibson, Les Massie, Kevin McHale and Gordon Low. A few weeks later Denis was covering a second leg League Cup match against Nottingham Forest for Radio 2 at Leeds Road; on seeing me, he got up from his seat, shook my hand and said 'Yes, Eddie Boot, I remember now'.

The meetings on the third Monday in the month were so successful that it was decided to have an annual dinner each November; until the new stadium was built, these events were held at the hotel at Ainley Top which kept changing its name.

Nat Lofthouse, the Lion of Vienna and former Bolton and England centre forward, was the guest speaker in the Living Legend spot and he asked me if I saw him play; he was quite impressed when I reeled off the Bolton Wanderers forward line; Holden, Moir, Lofthouse, Hassall and Langton followed by the rest of the team. In the room that evening were Vic Metcalfe and Don McEvoy, a former Town centre- half, who played at the same time as Nat and I pointed them out.Nat made a note and when he was 'singing for his supper' commented that this would be the first time on visiting Huddersfield that he had not been kicked by Don McEvoy; this prompted Don to stand up and say ' There's time yet, Nat' Cue for the house to be brought down.

Tom Graveney, Geoff Headey (Chairman HTAFC) and Denis Law

Nat Lofthouse, Ian Darke, Gary Richardson and Goldie Goldsmith

Fred Trueman, Terry Fisher (HTAFC) Ron Yeats and Stan Taylor

Keith Wilde and Gordon Taylor (PFA)

A group of Sporting Club members with Sir Richard Hadlee

Howard Kendall, Mick Budden and Paul Markham (HT Sporting Club)

Chris Hassall (far left) with Sporting Club members John Merriman and John Metcalfe

Don Wilson and Trevor Booth (Sporting CLub member)

Robert Denman and Chris Kamara

Craig Brown, former manager of Scotland, with a Sporting Club member in front of the trophy presented to HTAFC for winning the Championship in 1924/5/6

John Morgan (HT Sporting Club) Peter Maloney, Duncan McKenzie
and Billy Wright

David Ansboro (Guest) Peter Swales (Chairman Manchester City)

David Gower signing his benefit year book with Chris Patzeit (HTAFC)

Robert Whiteley (Director HTAFC) Malcolm McDonald and Keith Walker (HT Sporting Club)

David Gunson, Christopher Martin – Jenkins, Gordon Banks and George Binns (HTAFC)

Also on the top table that evening were Ian Darke and Gary Richardson who re-enacted their shows which were popular on the radio; they used topical material and then added ' There has been a late goal at Old Trafford where Nat Lofthouse has scored an equaliser for Bolton'. They then looked across at Nat and said 'Blimey, it must have been late'

Another year Fred Trueman filled the Living Legend spot with a supporting cast of Ron Yeats and Stan Taylor, a raconteur who had people in stitches when recalling the exploits of a submarine captain who had run out of torpedoes. Ron, a huge man, confirmed that he and Ian St John were first approached by Bill Shankly when he was Town's manager but apparently finance was the problem; if only! Ron and Ian became two of Shanks's early signings when he moved to Liverpool. As far as I am aware, a photograph of the speakers together with Town chairman Terry Fisher is still on display in the boardroom.

Back at Leeds Road, the largest attendance was for Bobby Charlton – it was a scramble for the buffet that evening. When the name of Billy Bremner came up, there were some rumblings of discontent from certain members of the committee in that he had played for that lot in LS 11 but sporting sense prevailed and we all thoroughly enjoyed a very entertaining performance. Sometimes it was a question of getting speakers when they were available;

Malcolm McDonald was snapped up soon after his appointment as Town manager as the committee did not think he would be in the hot seat for long – he wasn't.

Gordon Taylor, now PFA chairman, told how he was rejected by Mick Buxton who said he wanted someone younger and with more pace. On the cricketing side we were fortunate to engage some of the leading players when they were having their benefit years. David Gower, Allan Lamb and Richard Hadlee all came armed with their souvenir brochures. Richard Hadlee was a bit worried about the question and answer session.During the interval I told him that someone would probably ask him to name a team made up of the best players in his era and he duly jotted down some names. Sure enough the question came up and, sotto voce, he thanked me.

The move to the new stadium brought a problem on the catering front in that the magnificent buffets, famous for a dozen years, could not move with the Sporting Club. Unfortunately the first effort by the stadium staff was a disaster and there was trouble in t'camp. George Binns then came up trumps by negotiating a deal whereby we got meat and potato pie with mushy peas (mint sauce also).From then on, Sandra knew not to make anything at tea-time when it was the third Monday in the month.

In 1982 the Sporting Club was the only place in the area where you could hear and speak to the sporting personalities of that time; gradually other organisations cottoned on to what could be money-spinning events. This competition together with Sky Television showing a live match and the fact that the players who had just retired did not need the money as much as their predecessors caused problems. As fees to speakers went up membership numbers declined and in January 2005 the last Monday evening meeting was held. For over 20 years, the Sporting Club had provided funds to the football club and countless hours of enjoyment to its members.

The annual dinner continues to flourish with the top speakers in the land attracting sell out attendances.

CHAPTER 24

Badminton

When Sandra and I moved to live in Appleton Roebuck in 1970, the only person whose name I had heard of was Bert Tait, a friend of one of my work colleagues Arthur Milling; it was very convenient that Bert was the landlord of the Shoulder of Mutton. After Bert and I had almost exhausted the subject of football and his beloved York City in particular, we moved on to current sporting issues. Bert was a member at Bishopthorpe Badminton Club and invited me to a club night; I had not played before but with my natural eye for a ball (or feather in this case) soon got into the swing of things and decided to join.

This was an all male club but occasionally, to give us all a treat, Gordon Bean would bring along his wife, the delectable Beryl. There were two club nights each week and club had two teams in the local men's doubles league. Club nights started at 7pm and ended in the Woodman Inn somewhat later following several pints of bitter to provide mental sustenance for the games of fives and threes. Concentration levels had to be high as there was 50p at stake.

Each league team was made up of three pairs meaning there were nine rubbers in a match with only one court at home, this meant a late finish. It took me quite a while to convince Sandra that we had not been in the pub. Some clubs had two or three courts but Sandra was not aware of this.

We used to get the usual thrashing whenever we played Railway Institute who attracted players from all over the district as they had teams in a higher league where the standard was quite high. I recall we arrived on one occasion much to the surprise of John Bellerby, the RI Fixture Secretary. John had somehow not noted the match on his list of fixtures but completely unperturbed soon rounded up five volunteers to make up his team; needless to say the score was the familiar 9-0.. However with three courts available, the massacre was soon over and the beer was cheap in their club bar.

One evening not forgotten in a hurry was the long trip to Howden where there was only one court which at one end sloped down from the net to the end wall. At first there was a problem running backwards giving the home team a tactical advantage. I was one of the car drivers and as luck would have it, was involved in the last rubber. I was the only member of our team not to go to the pub between games which as things turned out was fortunate. When we got to the car to set off home, I found my battery was flat. After a push I managed to get the engine going but realised I was rapidly approaching the A63 which at the time ran through the middle of Howden and so I decided to reverse the 50 yards back down this narrow street. My driving was immaculate and this was confirmed by two gentlemen who had just emerged from a car on top of which was a flashing blue light. When I explained the position and told them how far we had to travel, they let us go but with the warning that next time I came to Howden, would I please not reverse 50 yards in the wrong direction down a one way street.

Another tricky venue was the court at Rowntrees which had a low ceiling. The local ruling was that the point would be played again if the feather hit the roof on your opponents' side of the net. The matches always took longer because it was so tempting to whack the ball up to the ceiling if the rally was going pear-shaped. At Sutton on Derwent not only was the ceiling low but there was not much room down the sides. Terry Smith rushed across the court to return the feather with his backhand, misjudged the flight and instead hit a rather flimsy curtain which went over the net. Meanwhile the feather landed just outside the court and it was our point. To which Terry said ' I was going to leave it anyhow'

It was with some reluctance that I stopped playing badminton but other interests and a family growing up rapidly meant I really did not have sufficient time to spare.

CHAPTER 25

Golf

There was no tradition for the game of golf in our family. In the 1950s and 1960s it appeared to be a rich man's sport with the fees being beyond the means of the average working man. Fortunately times have changed. In the early 1970s I met Mick Wing or to give him his full name Michael Anthony Thomas Wing, thus explaining why he sometimes answered to the name of Matt.

David Addinall (far right) with partners at a Charity Event in Leeds

Matt lived at the top of North Field Way and beyond his house was an open field where my first golf lesson took place. I seemed to pick up the basics quite well and in my lunch hour during the week went to the driving range. Interest was clearly growing and when Arthur Milling, the horticultural and agrochemical manager at Hargreaves Fertilisers saw me with the odd clubs I had borrowed from Matt suggested that I apply to join Pike Hills Golf Club as he supplied products to keep the greens in good order.

One of my work colleagues, David Addinall, was also interested in golf and our applications for membership went in together; meanwhile David and I used to practice in the huge back garden of a house which belonged to Bert Tait. David had a Japanese six iron which despatched the ball a huge distance when a good contact was made.

I went for interview at the Golf Club which was controlled, via a committee, by British Rail and was admitted as an 'external' member. I think Arthur and Bert had had a word with Bert's son Peter who was on the committee and it was put to me that would it be awkward for me if my application was accepted and others refused. David. Matt and I played as members the next weekend. Later we were joined by another resident of Appleton Roebuck, George Stowe.

I bought a half set of matched clubs from the pro, Gregor Love, and also arranged some lessons. We played regularly on Sunday mornings, winter and summer. In the middle of the course is a Nature Reserve, Askham Bog, and often in the winter months we played off temporary tees and greens. One particular Sunday morning the course was 'rather damp' following heavy rain and at 07.45 a light snow shower had developed. Greg wanted to close the course and said 'Have none of you got wives to go home to?' To which the reply from one of the assembled company was 'Have you seen my wife?'. I plead not guilty.

I entered the Rabbits Knock Out, a competition for players with handicaps of eighteen or over.At the time the maximum was twenty four – my handicap. It was a sunny Tuesday evening and I was absolutely slaughtered 7 and 6 by a youth who did not even have the courtesy to accept my offer of a drink in the bar afterwards. Next year I drew a guy called Ted who usually played in a four in front of us on a Sunday. At the time the rail unions from time to time went on a go slow and Ted's group were known as the ASLEF four. No prizes for guessing why – was it really necessary to line up a putt from every possible angle on a temporary green!

Once again the weather was kind and on the evening of our match, the course was busy and so we teed off at a hole part way round; it was 18 holes after all. Drives stayed on the fairway from where irons shots found the greens and the putts sank. I was five up with eight to play and was in cloud cuckoo land. Ted was a dogged competitor and went on to win the next six holes. One down with two to play and somehow I clawed my way back into the game by scrambling a par 4 at the penultimate hole. It was all on the last which, because we had not started on the first hole, was the short par three by the side of the car park and clubhouse.

My seven iron off the tee looked good until it developed a slight hook and landed just out of bounds. I played a second ball which ended up a foot from the pin. Ted needed a par to win the titanic contest but left his tee shot short; nerves were creeping in. I wonder how Peter Allis would have described the scene. His approach to the green was a tad heavy, leaving him an awkward downhill putt of five feet. As the saying goes 'There's a lot of golf in that one yet'. Would I get a reprieve or would it be a case of defeat snatched from the jaws of victory. Ted crouched, got up and had another look and another and finally struck the ball which careered towards the hole. It struck the far side of the lip, did two laps of honour and dropped.

'Blast' I thought – or similar words- but went over to Ted to congratulate him. We enjoyed a couple of pints and parted the best of mates. Which is what the game is all about?

One of the problems of playing on the home club course each week is the predictability; from the tee I tended to fade the ball with a wood and on the fairway to hook with an iron. This meant I got to know some parts of the course rather well. It was a pleasure to play with the Hargreaves Golfing Society during summer evenings. I played well at Pannal, had a disaster at a windy Howley Hall and, after going round Scarcroft, enjoyed the pie and pea supper more than the golf.

Our usual Sunday round finished before the nineteenth was open to sell alcoholic drinks and so we used to persuade the genial Fred, the steward, to serve up three cups of coffee. We had all played quite well one day and in a fit of enthusiasm decided to have a weekend away in Scotland. David made all the arrangements and we invited along Dick Hallaways, a work colleague at Hargreaves Fertilisers, despite the fact that he was a bandit off 24 handicap.

Mick had the largest car. He was the manager of the York branch of a national company specialising in motor finance and had to look the part. One Friday morning we set off from Appleton Roebuck, bombed up the A1 and arrived at Berwick on Tweed golf club for lunch followed by 18 holes dominated by Dick. The golf was very enjoyable particularly when we were playing a hole where the green was not visible from the tee and we gave Dick the wrong marker to aim for. Unusually for Dick he sliced his tee shot and ended up on the correct fairway after all.

After a cup of tea we continued up the A1 to North Berwick where we were staying at the Bentleys House Hotel. David had commented he had got a good rate and it transpired that following a spate of murders in the area, a body had been found in the boot of a car abandoned in the hotel car park. The evening meal was excellent and after a couple of pints in one of the several bars in this seaside resort we slept well.

The next day we played the East course in the morning and I remember Mick had a disaster on one hole where the green was on a plateau. We had all managed to reach the green apart from Mick whose ball had stopped half way up a steep slope. All he had to do was to chip 5 yards on to the green but he had already played one more shot and so I suggested he took his putter in an effort to get down in one. Mick was not sure but was easily persuaded and after much fuss over lining up his shot checked his stance. Unfortunately he did not keep his head down and scuffed the ball which did not reach the top of the slope and began to trickle back towards Mick. The look on his face was a picture as the ball gathered speed and ended up 20 yards further back from where it had started. It was difficult not to laugh and David, Dick and I failed miserably.

A local fish and chip restaurant provided a superb lunch and in the afternoon we tackled the East course again. At the infamous hole Mick got on the green in two with an excellent nine iron from 60 yards, sank the putt for a birdie and just smiled. He didn't need to say anything as the expression on his face said it all.

Sunday morning was the big test as David had managed to book the tee for 8.30 on the West Course which had Championship status. This meant we had to arrange with the hotel manager for an early breakfast. He was used to such requests and did us the full English or should it be the full Scottish. Thus fortified, we walked the short distance to the starter's hut to find there was a huge crowd milling around; imagine 20 golfers with trolleys. When the call came in a Scottish brogue 'Mr Addinall's party to the tee please' I was terrified. With the waves from the North Sea crashing on to the beach some 20 yards away and under the scrutiny of a host of golfers who would all be better players than me, I took a 3 iron and was mightily relieved when the ball went down the middle and landed just short of a ravine which cut across the fairway. From there it was a five iron to the green, two putts and what a start. Par on the first hole. From then on it was downhill until the 18th which I also did in par. What an experience on a tough golf course which really exposed my deficiencies – a pity about the sixteen holes in the middle of the round. The two better players in our group, David and Dick, fared much better than Mick and me.

We went back to the hotel for lunch before the journey home. It was abundantly clear that all the other customers had been to church and were dressed in their Sunday best whereas we were in 'smart casual'. The hotel manager served us with pre-lunch drinks and said ' Have you gentlemen been to the kirk this morning?' knowing full well where we had been. Mick, having recovered from the trauma of the West Course, came up with a superb response.'No but we were on our knees praying more than once'.

At some point, I think it was the late 1970s, a change of ownership of the golf course was agreed and while not sure of the details, was perturbed when the membership fee was doubled to help with a down payment. This prompted an audit of my sporting commitments with two daughters now in their teens and I decided that from a time and financial aspect, something had to go. I was playing cricket, getting involved in tennis and watching Huddersfield Town. The financial axe fell on golf as well as my membership of Yorkshire County Cricket Club, which at the time was really a debating society with Geoff Boycott as the sole subject.

I had never got to grips with golf as cricket and football reigned supreme. Playing only once a week does not improve your game and I did not feel sufficiently confident to go to the club and ask to make up a four. I did play another match however when I was Chairmen of the Institute of Chartered Secretaries (West Yorkshire Branch).I felt obliged to join in the annual golf tournament to be held at Horsforth. Once again I started well by getting a par at the first hole but then I began to think about the game. The result was an inept performance which confirmed that my decision to abandon any golfing ambitions was correct.

CHAPTER 26

Playing Cricket: School to 1954

I first held a cricket bat when playing on the path in our back garden in New Street, Farsley. I suspect that elder brother Jim (by six years and two days) was told to keep me occupied and we took it in turns to bat and bowl. As the path was only five yards long the 'bowler' would actually throw the ball in a way similar to that used by players in the first class game when warming up. This enabled the 'bowler' to impart spin as the tennis ball would grip on the concrete surface.

I bat right handed and my brother would set a natural attacking field when doing his impression of Ellis Robinson, the Yorkshire off-spinner. Natural was the operative word. At silly point was a privet hedge while his leg trap consisted of four gooseberry bushes which may not have produced much fruit but they could certainly catch a tennis ball.Many a time the entry in the scorebook would have read 'caught gooseberry bush 1 – bowled elder brother' In fact those gooseberry bushes were almost as efficient as Brian Close fielding in the leg trap at Park Avenue, Bradford when Ray Illingworth was bowling.

With my brother Jim at the wedding of Karen in 1988

At primary school we played in the play area provided where we had a pitch of 18 yards. We had to take our own equipment and so anyone with his own bat got a knock early on as did someone with a newish tennis ball or one made of a composite rubber substance. As the war had only just finished, the lack of equipment meant there was no official school team. However the top class(the oldest ones) challenged the rest of the school to a 'Test Match' and Mr Shepherd, who before the war had played for Doncaster Rovers, arranged to use the field at Farsley Cricket Club who also lent us some bats, pads and a ball. Their stars were Smiler Walker, Dudley Williams and Tony Brayshaw but none of them got going and we bowled them out for about eighty. The pitch was right on the edge of the square at the bottom end of the ground which meant there was a short boundary and our opening batsman, John Hudson made the most of it; their bowlers could not maintain a good line as John was left handed. The match was virtually won when I went in at number 5 and we triumphed by 7 wickets. It was a surprise result which was mentioned at assembly the next morning by Mr Nolan, the Headmaster.

A group of us in the school holidays would go to the cricket field and play 'little cricket' on the edge of the outfield. The pitch was 10 yards with no fast bowling or big hitting.On reaching 15 runs, a batsman had to bat left handed (or right handed as was the case for John Hudson). Someone who wanted to win – I plead guilty – batted left handed first and then changed after scraping 15 runs. I declared on reaching my century and prompted a change in the rules.

I left primary school before a cricket team was formed and went to Bradford Grammar School where I played in the under 14 side; this was the

Bradford Grammar School Under 14 X1 1951
Mr Locket, G Ormondroyd, P Bailey, R Fieldhouse, R Appleyard, I Presto, C Whelan, P North, a Gray, T Day, I Hewitt, M Stocks, A Webster and J Waterhouse

first time I had come across an organised outfit. On the Friday before the first match we were asked to report to the cricket field where Mr Lockett, who taught Physics, told us how to present ourselves in the field. The skipper, Ian Hewitt, was told to nominate his opening bowlers and to agree at which end each would bowl. Every bowler was instructed to have his field placings in his head if called upon by the skipper.

The fielder at third man would become mid on for the next over; cover point may cross the pitch and slips would follow the wicket keeper. Each bowler was told to go back to his run up when the ball was dead so that as the ball was returned to him via mid off, he ready to bowl the next delivery. This paid dividends, as our opponents the next day were a complete shambles compared to us. We remained undefeated in 1951 season with all the players after leaving school featuring in local league cricket. The pick of the bunch were Gordon Ormondroyd who went to Lightcliffe, Tony Webster with Farsley and Pudsey St Lawrence, Robert Fieldhouse with Bowling Old Lane, Adrian Gray who played Minor Counties cricket and Michael Stocks who represented Guiseley as wicket keeper/batsman for many years. In one match that season my bowling analysis read 7 overs, 7 maidens four wickets for no runs – all were stumped off my 'floater' by Nobby.

The success continued during the next season, although we had a bit of a scare when travelling to Skipton GS. We had taken the service bus on a very humid day for a match played on a Wednesday with most of us grabbing a sandwich to eat on the way.In conditions ideal for swing bowling we were put in to bat and soon lost four quick wickets and when I went in at Number 6 my instructions were not to get out. I remember three cover drives of which Len

Bradford Grammar School Second XI 1954

Hutton would have been proud and when the inevitable storm came bringing torrential rain, my partner and I had moved the score along to over 70. My individual score was twenty something not out – good for the average!

After playing in under 14 and under 15 teams, 1954 brought open age cricket with more competition for places in the three sides. I started in the third team but after a few games won a place in the seconds. My last outing for the third team was at Ilkley GS where after being put in to bat on a sporting pitch we only mustered 106.The home side dealt with the conditions better and at 106 for 6 looked set to win. However one batsman had a rush of blood and was run out and when another wicket fell in the same over, it was game on. The batsman who had been watching the debacle from the non-striker's end then got a ball which almost went underground to well and truly 'castle ' him. The last man approached the crease nervously but just as the previous wicket had fallen to a delivery which never got off the ground, this poor guy got one that lifted off a length. Fielding at gully I dived to my left to take a spectacular one-handed catch and the game was tied. Possibly that was the moment my promotion to the second eleven was sealed.

The rest of the season was uneventful and brought to an end my schoolboy cricket. I did play in one more match that season when I was asked to make up the numbers in the second team at Farsley in a fixture against Bradford. Eric Hill, the skipper, asked me what I bowled to which I replied off spin as I thought I had more chance of getting on rather than saying slow medium. When the opportunity came, I soon realised that I could not put enough spin on the ball and reverted to slow medium while still having a field set for off spin. After four reasonably economical overs without looking as if I would ever take a wicket, Eric, quite rightly, took me off. My bowling performance was a shambles but I did take a good catch in the outfield.

CHAPTER 27

Pudsey Britannia 1955

With Huddersfield Town doing well in the First Division, I did not give any thought to cricket until mid May. I was working for Midland Bank in Leeds often not getting away until 1pm on a Saturday. This meant I could not play for Farsley in the Bradford League as it would have been difficult to get to home games on time using public transport and therefore impossible to travel to Bingley and Lightcliffe.

About half way through the season, I was reading the Pudsey and Stanningley News and realised that Pudsey Britannia played in the Leeds League. I didn't know anyone there but one Tuesday evening dusted off my cricket boots and turned up at the nets. I was made very welcome and after a couple of weeks was selected to play for the second team away at Hunslet Nelson. On asking where the ground was, I was told to catch a number 1 tram, get off at the Swan Junction, go down the road on the left, cross the road with some huge advertising hoardings on the left and, on reaching the Guinness advert go through a door beyond which was the home of Hunslet Nelson. At the time there was a great deal of heavy industry in South Leeds but I was utterly amazed to find that the field was a dirty yellow colour instead of green.

I found the changing room and was relieved when some of my team mates arrived. Most of them had been here before and knew what to expect. Apart from meeting people at the nets, the only person I knew was Tom Hart who lived in Farsley. His father had a chemist's shop on Town Street between the Conservative Club and Lambert's Garage. The skipper was a small, stout, balding gentleman called LP (Leonard) Gaunt who was a solicitor in Pudsey. Our opening bowlers kept the run rate down but one of the opening batsmen, a large man who batted left handed, cut loose with a three fours and it was time for a change. I was agreeably surprised when LP tossed the ball to me. This time I was organised and with help from LP and Tom got my field set correctly went round the wicket to the left hander and fired the first two deliveries in making sure he could not score. I could sense his frustration. He ought to be carting this little lad out of the field. The next ball was tossed higher, pitching about six inches outside off stump and turning away towards the slips. The batsman took a mighty swipe but got a thick edge, nevertheless with his power the ball flew up into the air. Fortunately Tom had placed our best fielder at deep extra cover and he pouched it – my first wicket.

From then on, it was a procession as batsman after batsman committed hari kari and I ended up with 7 wickets for 21 and Nelson, after a promising start were all out for eighty something. It was the custom in those to take a collection from the spectators for a bowler who took 6 wickets for under 36 runs but I was in dreamland and didn't notice a little man going round with his cap. No doubt this was partly because there were less than a dozen people witnessing my feat – plus one dog.

We always looked like winning and when I went in to bat at number 7 the scores were level. A few minutes later it was all over and I hadn't faced a ball. The Club provided the equipment i.e. bats, pad and gloves and it was the duty of the not out batsmen to pack the large bag. Tom lent a hand and the bag was placed in the boot of someone's car. Although I was only seventeen I was then propelled, reluctantly I would say, to the Swan where our victory was to be celebrated. I was hardly through the door when one of my team 'mates' shouted 'Here he is' to the landlord who then asked me for 2 shillings and sixpence. Apparently the collection did not cover a round of drinks and I had to make up the difference. That was my first taste of Tetley's bitter and certainly not the last. There was no doubt this was a spectacular debut and as my cricketing career unfolded there are to be several other debuts of note. The match the following week was at home and I took 2 wickets for 35 against Thrift Stores.-a performance which was to earn me promotion to the first team.

Tom told me a story about LP which I think is worth telling even though I was not present at the match in question. I consider the integrity of my informant to be impeccable. One very hot day LP lost the toss and Britannia were asked to bat on a hard bumpy pitch which was prepared, or under-prepared, for the two opening bowlers for the home side. Wickets tumbled but LP remained at the crease. No doubt because he contrived to avoid the strike as often as possible. Eventually one of the Trueman like bowlers hurt his ankle and had to leave the field. His replacement, apparently, was the son-in- law of the skipper who clearly was guilty of nepotism. The new bowler trundled up some slow medium tripe and a young man batting at number 7 smashed the first three balls to the boundary. He looked down the pitch to see a red-faced and irate LP bouncing down the pitch towards him like an animated blackcurrant in a Ribena advert. The gist of the one way conversation was that LP wanted to get some runs off this bowler before he was banished to the outfield. Consequently the young man played the next three deliveries with great respect drawing a favourable comment from the skipper to his son in law who was to get another over when it had been contrived that LP was on strike. After struggling with the opening bowlers here was his big opportunity to score some easy runs. He rushed down the pitch intending to smash the ball out of sight, misjudged whatever flight there was and was stumped. The incoming batsman muttered 'Hard luck LP' while the rest of the team decided to have a walk round the boundary edge where their laughter would not be heard.

After the successful debut in the second team, my initial appearance for the first eleven was also dramatic and started the trend of impressive debuts. The opponents at the Britannia ground were Leeds Police; they batted first and I took 6 wickets for 64. This would have been better but I took a lot of stick in my last two overs when Police were having a bit of a go as their overs were running out.

Nevertheless I was delighted, particularly as we won the match. My ability with the bat was not tested.

My next memory was the final match of the season against Kirkstall Educational. We had just missed out on promotion and they were in mid-table. On a dry dusty pitch we batted first and got less than a hundred – my contribution was a duck. Misjudging the flight, I lifted my right heel and the wicket keeper made a smart stumping.The bowler was Tommy Cooper who was an experienced slow left armer who regularly featured prominently in the league averages. On the day he did his average no harm at all by taking six wickets for not many.

We didn't have much to bowl at but got an early breakthrough. I was brought on sooner than I expected presumably because if I had a bad over, there was more time for the team to recover. After all I was still a novice at this level. In my first over I was carted for six on the leg side but two balls later when I saw the batsmen coming down the pitch, I managed bowl wide of the off stump and Foster Holmes, our wicket keeper did the necessary.

With no margin for error in defending a small total, I was given another over in view of the fact that a wicket had fallen and I would be bowling at a new batsman. On the bowler – -friendly pitch I was turning my off spinners and did as Tommy Cooper had done by taking six wickets. We won the match with not many runs to spare. This time the collection money did pay for a round of drinks.

CHAPTER 28

Pudsey Britannia 1956

Expectations were high as Eric Vevers was returning to the club after a successful season as a professional at Batley where he took 44 wickets at an average of 13.08. His professional contract was earned as a result of his performances at Britannia in 1954 when he claimed 65 victims at an average of 7.5. With a strong pace attack of Eric supported by Geoff Gornall and Neville Naylor, Jack Myers and Derek Bean, there were no easy wickets to be had but at the end of the season I had bowled 118 overs and taken 18 wickets for 360 runs.

Following one memorable match against Gildersome Eric Vevers and I made the headlines; Eric took 6 for 13 and I backed him up with 3 for 13 although I did get their top scorer caught and bowled for 19 out of their total of 50. I had to catch that one or I would have suffered severe damage to my anatomy. In addition to the local papers, our names appeared in the News of the World which at the time was the Sunday scandal paper. We struggled to win the match, losing 6 wickets in the process.

We played three matches at Whitsuntide and won all of them; the headline in the Pudsey and Stanningley News read Britons in the Sun. On the Saturday we were at Colton and for once our opening attack did not get the usual early breakthrough. Nev Naylor and I toiled away on a hot day and eventually Nev broke the opening stand and soon got another. I chipped in by getting three of the middle order before Eric returned for a second spell taking the last 5 wickets at a cost of a mere 6 runs. The Colton total of 122 was clearly not enough and we won the match by 5 wickets with Grenville Fletcher holding the innings together with 42 not out.

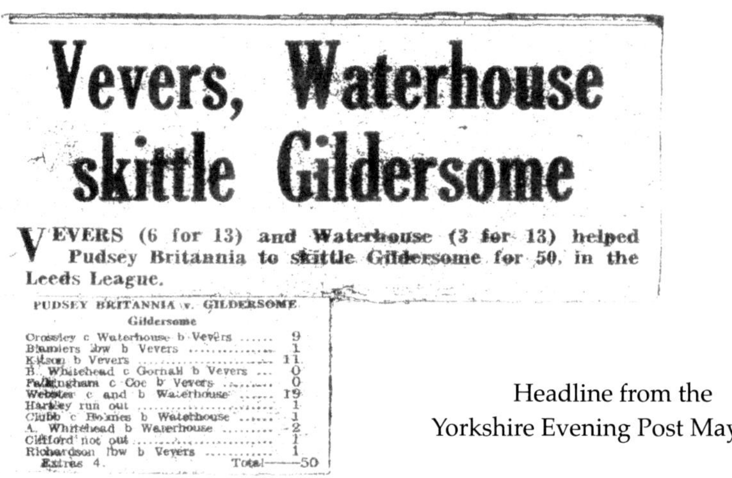

Vevers, Waterhouse skittle Gildersome

VEVERS (6 for 13) and Waterhouse (3 for 13) helped Pudsey Britannia to skittle Gildersome for 50, in the Leeds League.

PUDSEY BRITANNIA v. GILDERSOME

Gildersome

Crossley c Waterhouse b Vevers	9
Blamiers lbw b Vevers	1
Kitson b Vevers	11
B. Whitehead c Gornall b Vevers	0
Falkingham c Coe b Vevers	0
Webster c and b Waterhouse	19
Hartley run out	1
Clubb c Holmes b Waterhouse	1
A. Whitehead b Waterhouse	2
Clifford not out	1
Richardson lbw b Vevers	1
Extras 4. Total	50

Headline from the Yorkshire Evening Post May 1956

The deadley duo - 53 years later

On Whit Monday, we played Carlton at home. They batted first scoring 158 for 8 with Geoff Gornall taking 4 wickets and Eric Vevers 2; my name did not appear in the report in the local paper and I can not remember whether I got on to bowl or not. Carlton had an opening bowler called Lightowler whose action was decidedly dodgy. Rumour had it that he had been banned from two leagues because of alleged throwing. Harold Coe, one of our opening batsmen, was clean bowled without making a shot.' I thought he had stopped' claimed Harold as Lightowler suspended his run up, bent his arm, despatched the ball and then trotted down the pitch as if completing his follow through. That was not the start we wanted but Les Bramham carried his bat for an unbeaten 70 and with Geoff Gornall hitting a quick 22, we won by 3 wickets. Lightowler took 5 of the 7 wickets to fall; I would have been the next man in.

Whit Tuesday saw a return to Colton in the Hepworth Cup. As in the league match on the previous Saturday, the home side batted first and scored

123. Eric Vevers, Geoff Gornall and I got three wickets each and there was a run out. At one stage when I was bowling, one of the batsmen was right handed and the other left handed for whom I switched to round the wicket. This meant the sightscreen had to be moved frequently and this was irritating the batsmen who kept muttering. I asked our skipper whether I should bowl over the wicket all the time.' Not b.....y likely' was his response' They'll get thissens out afore long' One of them did and we got the breakthrough Les Bramham (63) and Harold Coe (44) provided a good start and we won by 6 wickets

When we played at LICS, we lost the toss but, after getting a good score thought we would win against a team near the foot of the league. On a good firm pitch we were struggling to dismiss the middle order after an initial breakthrough. I replaced Eric Vevers and after one over realised that there was nothing in the pitch for me; no way would I get any turn with my off-spinners. Ronnie Ambler who lived in Pudsey, was digging in and so, with plenty of runs to play with, I decided to bowl a leg break out of the back of my hand. At practice in the nets this could be a long hop or a full toss but on this occasion the ball pitched on a length on leg and middle, spun away from the bat and just passed over off stump. Ronnie looked down the pitch as if to say 'What happened to that one ?'That proved to be the best delivery I bowled in my career despite the fact that it did not claim a wicket. We drew the match with LICS about 90 runs short of our total with nine wickets down; I did get a wicket with a leg break when an obliging batsman hit a long hop straight to deep square leg.

Coronation Cup Decider

G. GORNALL and young J. Waterhouse have been the other leading Pudsey bowlers.

In addition to his ability to puzzle batsmen with his spinners, Waterhouse is showing signs of developing as a run-getter.

He scored 16 not out last Sunday in a crisis when Britannia beat Farsley, the former club of his father, Mr. Donald Waterhouse, in the Coronation Cup.

Britannia will meet Pudsey St. Lawrence or Calverley in the cup decider

BOWLING (1956)

League and Cup Matches

	O	M	R	W	Av.
N. W. Naylor	89	27	189	27	7
E. Vevers	195.1	48	485	46	10.54
A. Smith	41.2	5	115	9	12.77
G. Gornall	185.1	35	477	33	14.45
J. H. Waterhouse	118.2	14	360	20	18.

5 wickets and under: J. Myers 12, 3, 16, 2, 8; D. Bean 11.3, 3, 20, 1, 20; M. Tobin 8, 0, 25, 1, 25.

July 1956 – Cutting from Pudsey and Stanningley News Pudsey Britannia bowling averages 1956

We just missed out on promotion to a comparative new club, Yorkshire Copper Works who beat us at home Defending a modest total of 123, they bowled us out for 86 using three slow left arm bowlers which was unusual at the time; our batting performance was criticised in the local paper as lacking concentration and conviction. In league and Hepworth Cup matches I bowled 118 overs and took 20 wickets at an average of 18; the leading wicket takers were Eric Vevers (46), Geoff Gornall (33) and Neville Naylor (27).

During the summer evenings the Midland Bank (Leeds branches) played matches against other organisations in the financial sector but the highlight was a fixture with Sam Smith's brewery at Tadcaster. We won a close match and the only contribution I made was taking a catch in the deep having run thirty yards to get there. My bowling and batting was deemed not suitable for 20 over cricket (the fore-runner of the 20/20 game) but I was a good fielder. We were entertained after the match in what is now The Angel and White Horse with some excellent sandwiches washed down with liberal quantities of beer.Just as our bus was about to leave, one gentleman whose name I will not reveal, decided that he needed to relieve himself and slipped out of the door without the driver noticing. Thinking that the bus provided sufficient cover he was doing what was necessary when the driver, not realising that we were one passenger short, set off towards the main road leaving our hapless colleague alone in the middle of the street which separates the two breweries. Sod's Law then came into play as two patrolling policemen walked down the main street and happened to look to their right.It took all of 20 minutes to persuade them not to report the incident and to let us get on our way.. Two months later, the culprit was promoted but what if.....?

During July the four local senior teams, Pudsey Britannia, Pudsey St Lawrence, Farsley and Calverley played in the Coronation Cup, a competition instituted at the behest of Pudsey Borough Council following the coronation of the Queen in 1953. We were drawn against Farsley at home; this was the first time my father who had played at Farsley for many years with distinction, saw me play. With a weakened side Farsley batted first and scored just over 100 in the forty overs allowed per side. I didn't bowl very well and according to my mother my field placings were all wrong. I was disappointed that my father, a very distinguished player and a highly qualified coach told her rather than me. With 6 overs to go I went into bat; there were 8 wickets down and still 30 runs required. My instructions were to let Foster Holmes have as much of the strike as possible but when Mike Fearnley sent up a half volley on off stump I despatched it through extra cover with a drive of which Len Hutton (or latterly Geoff Boycott)would have been proud. Growing in confidence I scored another 4 with a straight drive followed by a couple of delicate cuts which each brought two runs. One over to go and we needed 6 to win; Foster wasted no time. He hit the first ball into the nearby bowling green and we had completed the great escape. I finished up with 16 not out and scored as many runs as Foster in our match-winning partnership. The Pudsey and Stanningley News said I was developing into an all -rounder following that innings 'in a crisis'.

CHAPTER 29

Pudsey Britannia/National Service 1957 and 1958

I began my two year stint in the Army (National Service) in November 1956 and when the 1957 cricket season started I was at the RAOC camp at Blackdown, near Aldershot working as one of the permanent staff at a trade training unit. Shortly afterwards I moved to Bicester, near Oxford and so I played no cricket down there as, at the time, our battalion did not have a team; this was rectified the following year.

I managed to play eight matches at Britannia using week-end passes and annual leave. Surprisingly, I was second on the batting averages although this was a false position as I scored 41 runs in eight innings with six not outs. Billy Woolford topped the averages and also got most runs. I bowled 73 overs taking 14 wickets at an average of 18 which I thought was satisfactory as I had little time and no facilities to practice for most of the season.

In 1958 I was not able to travel back for as many matches and took five wickets for 79 in the first team who again just missed out on promotion. It was not fair to leave someone out of the first eleven to accommodate my sporadic visits and I played some games in the second team where, although there are no records available, I recall that my batting was more effective than my bowling.

I managed to play several games for the battalion team which was revived following the arrival of a Captain Coutts. He organised matches at various

Pudsey Britannia 1957 averages and preview of 1957 season

1957 Didn't play this season

BATTING AVERAGES

FIRST TEAM

	I	n.o.	R	Av.
W. Woolford ...	13	1	280	23.33
J. H. Waterhouse	8	6	41	20.5
D. W. Pae	6	1	128	[illegible]
D. Roo	9	0	135	[illegible]
L. Bramham	13	0	215	1[illegible]
E. Hargate	8	0	125	1[illegible]
K. Malett	12	1	130	1[illegible]
S. Briggs	8	0	107	1[illegible]
M. Tobin	6	2	50	12[illegible]
N. W. Naylor	13	2	130	11[illegible]
D. Bean	9	1	91	11.37
W. Waters	16	3	114	8.8
K. Lindley	15	1	85	6.07
P. Broadley	7	3	19	4.74
L. G. Fletcher	7	0	33	4.7
G. F. Holmes	5	0	22	4.4

BOWLING AVERAGES

1957

FIRST TEAM

	O	M	R	W	Av.
N. W. Naylor	197	40	481	45	10.7
D. Roo	114	20	327	22	14.86
D. Bean	92	16	263	17	15.47
P. Broadley	160	36	415	25	16.6
J. H. Waterh'se	73	13	252	14	18.00

It's A Trying Time For Britannia—

TOWARDS the end of last season Harold Coe left Pudsey to join Bowling Old Lane, and since then Eric Vevers who took 46 wickets for ten runs each in 1956, has gone to Pudsey St. Lawrence, while Geoff Gornall has moved to Farsley.

These departures have left big gaps and the position has not been improved by the call-up of young John Waterhouse, son of Mr. Donald Waterhouse, the Farsley stalwart.

1958

Our team of the week:

PUDSEY BRIT.

PUDSEY BRITANNIA TEAM.—Back row (left to right): S. R. Briggs, D. Roo, D. Wilson, P. Broadley, G. Gornall, J. Waterhhouse. Front row: D. W. Pae, W. Waters, L. G. Fletcher, L. Bramham, G. H. Holmes.

THEY HAVE BEEN 'NURSERY' FOR NOTABLES

military establishments to which we travelled in an army lorry. We enjoyed our visit to RAF Hermitage so much that a return trip was arranged – while the cricket was well contested between two teams of equal ability, the food was a distinct improvement on what was on offer at our camp. I recall one match at Wheatley Military Hospital when I took the final two wickets of their innings in the last over; both victims were caught by our wicketkeeper, a certain Captain Coutts, who bought the beer on the way home. Our home pitch was not fit to play on as it had been neglected for several seasons but our indomitable captain arranged to play on matting. We batted first and I carried my bat for 69 out of a total of 138. The ball came through slowly with an unpredictable bounce – I think the ground under the matting had not been prepared properly. Still we got a game in or half a game as after tea there was no play due to rain.

It has been said that truth is often stranger than fiction and I would say that the following report on events one Wednesday is a case in point. We had bowled out the Ox and Bucks Light Infantry for about 100 on a sporting pitch and, although we lost a couple of wickets early on, the cook sergeant from Todmorden and I were in control when he got an unplayable delivery and was bowled. As he was walking off the field I noticed a Military Police jeep sweep into the ground in a cloud of dust and two red caps heading to the dressing rooms. The incoming batsman who had started walking towards the middle, went back and got a message from the skipper (Captain Coutts was on leave) and then came over to have a word with me

The gist of the situation was that the MPs wanted me and I was to either get the winning runs quickly or get out. Fifteen runs were required and like Hurst and Rhodes some years before against Australia we got them in singles. I took a blow on the fingers but no way was I going to retire hurt.

When, eventually, we returned to the dressing rooms I was instructed to go with the MPs who would explain was happening. Apparently I was not in any trouble but was required to fly with a platoon of paratroopers to Cyprus early the following day; the plan was for me to interview captured terrorists and I had been chosen because of my knowledge of Greek. When I explained my O level was in ancient Greek, the MPs thought it was a huge joke but agreed to call at the Adjutant's quarters to see whether he could do anything to prevent what might have proved to be an expensive misunderstanding. The Adjutant didn't want to know and so we went to the Commanding Officer's house round the corner; Mrs CO said her husband had just left to meet the Brigadier for a drink. We all arrived at the brigade mess more or less at the same time. The Military Police jeep caused some concern. The Brigadier's first words were 'Did you beat the Ox and Bucks?' followed by ' You may be required for the brigade team next week, you can't go to Cyprus'

The upshot was that the Brig would do what he could but, as order were orders, I had to be prepared to travel early the next morning which meant packing all my gear. How delighted I was when the Guard Commander came to tell me at 05.30 hours that my trip had been cancelled- I had not had a wink of sleep-Well, you might say, What was all the fuss about? The plane was going to land in Cyprus but only after the platoon and their 'guest' had parachuted to some obscure spot in the Troodos Mountains. No doubt the usual eight week parachute jumping course would have been condensed to an hour.

CHAPTER 30

Kirkstall Educational 1959 to 1961

I completed my National Service on 20th October 1958 and I can still remember my army number: 23349497. After a week or so to become acclimatised to Civvy Street, I reported to the Midland Bank Training Branch for a refresher course, after which I was posted to the branch at 346 Kirkstall Road, Leeds. This was quite convenient as the West Yorkshire bus from Farsley to the city centre passed the door.

As regards sport, my mind was on football and Bramley Wanderers, rather than cricket when I bumped into Neville Naylor who had moved from Britannia to Kirkstall where he was born and lived for several years. The 'Eddies' were in the first division of the Leeds League and were looking for a bowler to back up their slow left-armer Tommy Cooper. I had no problems at Britannia and there was no reason for me to move but Neville persuaded me; it was a difficult decision to make.

My debuts with the second and then first teams at Britannia had been dramatic and the sequence was to be continued at Kirkstall. The opening match was against Claytons Sports who had the legendary Billy Newton in their team. I was told that Billy, now at the veteran stage of his career, had played as a professional in the Lancashire League when most of the other pros were former county or test players. Claytons batted first and were on the way to a reasonable score with about ten overs to go. I was quite satisfied with my performance at that point with four wickets bowling from the Queenswood Drive end and expected to give way to our pace man who had taken an early wicket in his opening spell. As if sensing that this would be his last chance to take advantage of a young slow bowler, the striker had a rush of blood and tried to hit a ball from outside off stump over the mid wicket boundary. The ball went high in the air and it looked at one stage as if it would go for six; however Bernard Butler, not the tallest of men, held on to the catch which meant in modern parlance that I had a 'Michele' (Pfeifer, film star – five for). The skipper, Dennis Pearse, came up to me, patted me on the back and said if the new batsman was on strike, I could have another over. He was and after the third delivery, Brian Cooper, our wicket-keeper, got a message to me that the batsman was standing outside his crease. The next ball was quicker, well pitched up and wide of the off stump; BC was ready and whipped off the bails to claim his first victim of the season.

Kirkstall Educational 1957
Maurice (?) Scorer, B Cooper, T Cooper, J Adamson, J Waterhouse, P Grey
B Butler, N Naylor, D Pearse, D Thorpe, A Wilkinson

Neville took a wicket in the next over from the bottom end and our opponents now had eight down. Dennis let me continue and once again, as the batsman was lured down the track, BC did the business. Neville wrapped up the innings in his next over. My figures were 7 for 42 – unbelievable! Billy Newton broke through the middle order and we ended up playing for a draw with seven wickets down. I was next man in.

Leeds Cricket Club operated two teams; one in the Yorkshire Council and another in the Leeds League. This meant there was a local match at Headingley every week, except when Yorkshire had a home fixture. Our big day came early in the season and I was delighted to see my seven wicket haul given a mention in the programme. Dennis Pearse had played with Leeds CC for several years and before we took the field, gave us some tips based on his experience. The square was rock hard and the ball would travel much quicker – a point for both fielders and batsman who were told not to play on the back foot until they had got accustomed to the pace of the pitch. Bowlers were advised to keep the ball pitched up as anything short would get hammered on what was usually a batsman's paradise. The groundsman had put us on the edge of the square towards the Western Terrace.

The format was 40 overs each and Leeds batted first. Their openers, Gray and Roberts, started well and after only eight overs I came on at the Kirkstall Lane end to take the pace off the ball and hopefully restrict the run rate. I certainly slowed the game down; Billy Roberts was a left hander and there were quite a few field changes as for both batsmen I bowled to a packed off side field pitching the ball on or outside off stump. There was no way I was going to get any turn and so I had to use change of pace and flight.

I went round the wicket for Billy and with the first ball of an over bowled a little quicker, just short of a length with the seam up. Billy played back and was beaten by the extra pace. The ball struck his pads bang in front of his stumps and he was plum LBW.The umpire, Billy Twigg, took ages to raise his finger. Apparently he had a reputation for not giving batsmen out LBW unless he was absolutely sure; in addition, he was a former Kirkstall player and I was bowling round the wicket. Dennis Thorpe came up from first slip and said it was the first time he could remember Billy giving an LBW decision in favour of a Kirkstall bowler. I was taken off with three overs to go at the Kirkstall Lane end having bowled 13 overs with my wicket which cost 41 runs. I was pleased with the economy rate as Leeds scored 206 for 3 in their allotted overs.

We lost three quick wickets and I when I went in to bat at the fall of the next wicket we were 4 down and had not reached 50 with the overs ticking by. The pitch suited my style of batting as I liked to get on the front foot; one cover drive brought a four and a push on the leg side produced two. My. confidence was sky high and that was my downfall; I went to drive a ball wide of off stump, got an edge and was caught at slip. Dennis Pearse came in next having dropped down the order to give us youngsters a chance and played a superb innings to be not out at the end with over 60 runs to his name. Once again we got a 'losing' draw finishing with seven wickets down and some thirty runs short. As for my batting performance all can say is that it was a wasted opportunity.

One of the top teams in the League was Holbeck; their stars were Jack Weatherill, the skipper, who had a spell at Farsley when my father was playing, and Horace Fisher, the former Yorkshire left arm spinner. They were backed up by some quality players such as Reg Parker, the wicket-keeper and Derek Walker, a stylish batsman who scored lots of runs. The home fixture was on 8th August 1959 which coincided with the wedding of Jim, my brother, and Avril; I worked it out that I could complete my best man duties and get a taxi to the ground in time. I made it. The start was delayed as one of the wheels of the sightscreen at the bottom end fell off and by the time a temporary repair job had been completed, I got on the field.

Holbeck had one or two players missing and our skipper asked them to take first knock on a hard, bumpy pitch. Our pace attack relished the assistance they got from the pitch and our visitors were skittled out for less than a hundred. My services with the ball were not required. During our innings there was an amusing incident. Holbeck were in disarray both on and off the field that day as they arrived without a scorer. Our regular 'notcher' was on holiday and his deputy was an enthusiastic youth who was most impressed when he was offered double pay if he kept both scorebooks going when Holbeck were fielding. He was not familiar with the names of the visiting players and when the distinguished figure of Horace Fisher came on to bowl he asked for the bowler's name in a loud penetrating voice. Most of the players could not conceal their laughter but HF was not amused. The young lad was probably the only person on the ground who did not recognise the former county player who still wore the Yorkshire sweater.

We scraped home by three wickets and I was not out 0 when my partner got the winning run.

Jim and Avril returned from their honeymoon and I told Avril I would remember the wedding day for a long time. She was not all that impressed when I said it was because Kirkstall had not beaten Holbeck for the first time in 14 years.

For the return match at Holbeck, in the shadow of the Elland Road football ground, the home team was at full strength. We were put into bat and struggled. With six wickets down and the overs passing by, I decided that a bit of aggression was called for. Using my feet, I played an immaculate cover drive off Horace Fisher and as the ball sped over the boundary I recalled my experience at Headingley earlier in the season. Sure enough the next delivery was well pitched up but wide of off stump; this time I left it alone. A couple of overs later I was facing Les Houldridge who bowled off spin; the first two deliveries were meant to prevent me scoring – just short of a length and a bit quicker. I anticipated that the next one would be given some air; it was and I hit it back over the bowler's head for an almighty six. In the next over, running out of overs and partners, I mis hit a drive into the covers and was caught. However no one can take away the satisfaction of two magnificent shots. We lost the match easily and I only got two overs in.

Another match to remember that season was the fixture at Lofthouse who were regularly challenging for the title. The sun shone brightly following rain in the previous day and their spin bowler from the pavilion end took most of the wickets on a pitch which was conducive to his type of bowling. Our total of around 120 did not seem enough and so the skipper decided to attack from the start.Tommy Cooper opened from the pavilion end; this was a masterstroke as wickets tumbled at regular intervals. One of the opening batsmen(we called him stonewall) defied all that Tommy could produce and remained a threat. I came on to support Tommy and started with a maiden over to 'stonewall', the afore mentioned opening batsman. We adopted the logical tactic of trying to keep the lower order batsmen on strike facing Tommy while I had to make sure 'stonewall' did not score from the last three balls of my over. Nine wickets were down when I started an over and decided to give the ball a little more air; pitching outside off stump as had most of my previous deliveries, the ball spun in sharply and trapped 'stonewall' plum LBW. Tommy took eight wickets and there was a run out- we had twenty runs to spare.

The practice facilities at Kirkstall, as with most league clubs at the time, were not very good and through a friend of my father's I became a member of Leeds CC; this meant that although I continued to play at Kirkstall, I could use the nets at Headingley which was only a five minute bus ride from where I was working. Several other players were doing the same as me and there seemed to be an open invitation to anyone in the Yorkshire Colts team to come whenever they wanted. The standard was high and I regularly had to fetch my ball from in front of the football stand; the nets were at the Kirkstall Lane end and it is a long way across the Headingley pitch, particularly the second or third time.

One of the characters was Arthur Clues, the huge Australian rugby league forward who played for Leeds. To add spice to practice Arthur would put a half crown piece on each stump; in real money each coin would buy a pint and a half of bitter. I never managed to castle Arthur but once I had him plum in front LBW but he refused to pay out – typical Aussie! Arthur was a great guy and regularly offered good deals on equipment at his sports shop in Leeds.

Kirkstall had a programme of Sunday fixtures which provided time in the middle for both batting and bowling. The first game of the season was a traditional fixture against Yorkshire Owls, a team of Bradford League professionals and players on the fringe of the Yorkshire Colts; we usually lost but I got satisfaction from two quality cover drives off the bowling of Colin Maston who went on to have a good season in the Bradford League. The Owls operated what nowadays would be termed a squad system with players dropping out in turn; there was no regular organised cricket in those days on a Sunday and when they were not in the selected eleven some players would turn up with their families, particularly if the match was at a picturesque country ground. To make a match of it and to enable the home club to run a raffle during the tea interval, it was generally understood that the Owls would bat first.

The story goes that on one occasion it was the turn of the opening fast bowler to drop out and he was persuaded to stand as umpire. The first delivery struck the batsman on the pad and there was a loud appeal. The local bowler said to the 'umpire' ' Well you appealed, how is he?''Bloody well out then' came the reply. I was not there but the story was repeated around cricketing circles and not denied by the person involved.

Another of the strong sides we met on a regular basis was Halifax Nomads and we were invited to enter a team in their annual five a side competition. We travelled in hope rather than expectation as some of the other sides were somewhat useful. We were on first and managed a narrow win. As there was a long wait for our next match we decided to visit the pub across the road and in so doing, disgraced ourselves by walking straight past the tables of sandwiches and pies provided free; I pleaded I was led astray as I was the youngest member of our team. We lost our next two games and were eliminated from the competition..I was bowled neck and crop by Chris Pickles who at the time was getting the odd game with Yorkshire.

My batting improved with extra practice as the summer progressed and I was robbed of my first half century at Whitkirk. We were facing a large total and, having had a bad start and then a middle order collapse, had no option but to play out for a draw. Somehow I had survived the mayhem and had about 25 overs to bat out. When I was in the thirties I hit a straight six but the umpire was not sure it had carried despite the puff of dust and signalled four; the nearest fielder, looking a bit sheepish, said he didn't see where the ball landed. Yes, you 've guessed it, I was out for 48.

CHAPTER 31

Farsley 1962 to 1964

In the summer of 1961, I was transferred from Kirkstall Road to a larger branch of Midland Bank at Market Street Bradford. I completed the season at Kirkstall travelling by train from Forster Square; this worked out quite well as the service to Leeds stopped at Kirkstall station.

I went to the nets at Farsley in the pre-season build up, hoping I would get a place in the second team. Imagine my amazement when I was selected in the first team for the opening match at home against Lightcliffe; apparently some of the regular players were not available.

Previous debuts with new teams had been dramatic and successful; my first match at Farsley was to ruin the sequence'. Lightcliffe batted first and their opening pair, after a slow start, began to move the score along. I thought I might get on first change but the skipper, Brian Claughton, decided to stay with pace and John Hainsworth got the nod. This was logical as the ball was still in good condition in view of the lush outfield.When my chance came, Harry Waterhouse, no relation, was still at the crease and going well. The pitch was on the top side of the square which meant that there was a long leg side boundary for a bowler from the Stoney

Brian Claughton

Royd end; this was to save me from severe punishment. I could not get my run up right and every delivery was short and after three overs of rubbish was prepared for the return to the outfield. Fortunately a wicket fell in the next over and with the new batsman on strike, I was given a reprieve. He looked as nervous as me which gave me a little hope. I decided to abandon the off spin and bowled seam up and a bit quicker. The ball got more bounce and brushed the batsman's glove on its way through to the wicketkeeper who, before I could appeal, dropped the catch. Dave Pullan, the regular keeper who went on to play for Nottinghamshire, could not play as he had damaged a finger and his stand in had no previous experience. The rest of the over was not bad only because I kept the rookie batsman on strike despite my run up problem. Quite rightly with Harry on strike for what would have been my next over, the skipper terminated my nightmare.

Needless to say I was in the second team the following week and at the end of the season had reasonable bowling figures of 96 overs of which 21 were maidens taking 20 wickets for 257 runs. In 1963 I bowled more overs, 168 with 25 wickets costing 472 runs. There were no amusing incidents to recall apart from hitting a straight six at East Bierley which struck a cow and caused a mini stampede, fortunately away from the cricket field.

In 1964, I was disappointed with my bowling; in 145 overs I took 19 wickets but they cost 464 runs. Over the three seasons not only did the cost of each wicket increase each year but the economy rate did also.

A match to remember, however, was down to my batting. Priestley Shield ties were played mid week starting on Monday evenings and we were drawn away at Idle. Their bowling attack was successful possibly due to the surprise element of opening with two fast left armers. We lost the toss and batted first on rain- affected pitch and a slow outfield. When bad light stopped play we were 110 for 8 after 42 overs with myself and Geoff Kay the not out batsmen. There was no play on Tuesday due to rain but Wednesday was a glorious day and by evening the pitch and the outfield had dried out.

A key point in the match occurred before play started. We commandeered their nets with Geoff and me facing our opening bowlers; the Idle players objected trying to quote some rule about not practising on the field during an innings. We ignored them and won a vital psychological battle

Incensed at what they thought was cheating, the opening bowlers knew they had only four overs each and were determined to polish off the innings as soon as possible. Accuracy was sacrificed for speed and when our innings closed after 50 overs, we had taken the score up to 148. In the context of the game for numbers 9 and 10 to add 38 runs at almost five runs per over against a fresh opening attack of much renown was remarkable at the time.

The Idle players after arriving at the ground in anticipation of an easy victory, now knew they had a fight on their hands. We had the psychological advantage and when we got both their openers out early we knew all we had to do was to bowl tight and the match was ours.All our bowlers did well and the wickets were shared out; excellent fielding with two superb catches being taken certainly helped.

In the end we won comfortably by 60 runs and found the Idle players arguing with each other and almost coming to blows. Apparently the reward for qualifying for the semi finals was a free trip to the Lyceum Club, a run down cinema converted into a casino and night club where the top entertainers appeared. Frankie Vaughan and Shirley Bassey were just two of the big names to take the stage. We lost to Lidget Green in the semi final but possibly we had already played our final in the previous round.

In 1962 the Bradford branches of Midland Bank were invited to play Head Office at the bank's palatial sports centre at Beckenham in Kent. This was scheduled for a Sunday. Play would commence at 11am and end at 6.30pm with breaks for lunch and tea. We travelled down on the Saturday which meant missing league matches for most of our team. After checking in at the Strand Palace hotel, we had a meal and then went to the Adelphi theatre to see the musical '76 Trombones.' The following morning we woke up to rain which had been forecast and travelled to Beckenham by train. We took an early lunch and Archie Knowles, our skipper, elected to bat on winning the toss. The plan was to get enough runs to be able to declare in view of the reduced playing time. Unfortunately our star man, Duncan Smith, who had played for Yorkshire Colts, was out early on and with another couple of wickets going down, I was promoted to stiffen the middle batting. We recovered – I got about 20 -and with a late flourish from the lower order, Archie was able to

Midland Bank – Bradford Branches v Head Office 1962

declare giving us time to bowl out the opposition while also providing them with a chance to win. In an exciting match they won by three wickets with less than ten minutes remaining and all the regulars at Beckenham, players and spectators, agreed it was the best game they had seen for a long time. Apparently visiting teams from the provinces usually made sure they didn't lose rather than go for the win which we had done.

In the bar afterwards we met some important figures in the bank including Mr Wood, one of the Joint General Managers who seemed surprised that we were all going to do a normal day's work on Monday. I arrived home at 4am and was not at my best when reporting for duty at the Market Street branch some four and a half hours later. I was asked by the Accountant, a person waiting to get on to the managerial ladder, how we had got on and was all smiles when I said we had made a good impression at Head Office. However his smile disappeared when I told him about Mr Wood's comment about not letting us have time off.

Sandra and I bought a house in Menston so as to be not far from where we worked in Guiseley and with no car, my short stay at Farsley was over.

CHAPTER 32

Burley 1965

Having more or less settled in at Menston, my thoughts turned to cricket and, was on my way to the nets at Menston CC one evening in April, when I saw a face which I thought I recognised. It turned out to be Jack Stocker who had played in the Bradford League against my father. Jack was still playing at Burley and persuaded me to join him there; as I didn't know anyone else at either Menston or Burley I agreed.

My performances at the nets went quite well and I was selected for the second team for the first match at Knaresborough. Once again there was an eventful debut. During the winter Knaresborough had sold their ground to a national house building company and moved across the road; however they transferred the turf from the square and re-laid it at the new ground. I opened the innings and was bowled by the second ball of the match which appeared to go underground and so I believe I hold the record of being the first batsman to lose his wicket at the new ground. What a start at a new club.!

The match became a lottery and we were all out for about 50; Knaresborough lost 8 wickets to win a low scoring game. The following week I got a few runs and a couple of wickets which resulted in promotion to the first team. I did nothing remarkable except on one occasion bowled six tight overs and on another held firm while the middle order collapsed. My fielding was good and I took several catches.

Harry Bolton skippered the side and I got on well with all the other players. I was quite content apart from the fact that I wanted to bat and bowl more.

We were drawn against Gargrave at home in the Waddilove Cup and in good conditions on the Monday evening scored over 220 runs in our allotted overs.

I was scheduled to bat at number seven but Harry kept promoting the big hitters and so I never got a knock. Our visitors batted on the Tuesday and we were conscious of the fact that one of their opening batsmen although at the veteran stage had played for Lancashire and had been scoring heavily in recent weeks in the division below us. Our opening bowlers were keeping the runs down which resulted in the required run rate gradually increasing. For once, Peter Hey bowled a ball short of a length outside off stump; the veteran went on the back foot and hit the ball hard on the off side; I stuck out an arm as the ball was on its way to the boundary,managed to stop it and then hit the stumps at the non-striker's end with a throw all of 25 yards. The star man was well out of his ground and we had the breakthrough.

The match was going our way when there was a sharp shower and we were off the field for 20 minutes. This didn't affect the overs but the ball was like a piece of soap and, ironically at this point, I was asked to bowl – presumably as a reward for my fielding. The idea was to take the pace off the ball. Clearly bowling off spinners was not on and I decided just to try bowling a good length. My first three overs were reasonably economical but the last two balls of the fourth went for 4 and 2 and the skipper made a change. With only ten overs to go Peter Hey,having had a rest,was brought back on. He had to bowl the last over with 36 runs needed for victory for Gargrave and with no restrictions on field placings, Harry had everyone back on the boundary. One wag behind me commented that six sixes would do it which was stating the obvious but when the first two deliveries sailed out of the ground, none of us were laughing. The third ball soared high into the darkening sky; the catch was taken and we had won.

A couple of weeks afterwards I decided to stop playing in that the best part of Saturday was taken up with cricket – fielding rather batting and bowling. With baby Karen to look after, decorating and a garden which wanted attention, I needed to spend more time with Sandra at home.

CHAPTER 33

Menston 1966 to 1968

In the spring of 1966, I decided to do what I should have done a year earlier and joined Menston CC. It was where we lived and Sandra could come and go as the ground was within walking distance of our house in Cleasby Road.

Once again there was drama on my debut with the now disastrous trend being continued. We had been bowled out for 64 by Horsforth Hall Park and when they wanted six runs to win with plenty of wickets in hand, I was asked to bowl at the Fox end by the skipper David Howarth. The leg side boundary was much shorter as the pitch was on the edge of the square. The most difficult thing about bowling is actually getting on to bowl in the first place, I was determined to do well in what would probably be a brief spell. It turned out to be the shortest possible when, after taking care setting my field, Neville Kempton who had the reputation of being a dour opening batsman, carted a ball from six inches outside off stump over the mid wicket boundary. My analysis was 0.1 overs, no maidens, 6 runs and no wickets. What made matters worse was that the non – striker was Peter Hargreaves, a former colleague at both Farsley CC and Bramley Wanderers AFC who thought it was a huge joke. I suppose after that the only way was up but the following week we were routed by Guiseley and were all out for 24 out of which David Storr scored 17. I was not out for nought and didn't get on to bowl. There was an ironic comment from a Guiseley player and work colleague at Crompton Parkinson John Whitaker when he pointed out that not only was the Fox and Hounds not open but it had only just closed from the lunch time session.

Although I kept my place in the first team, my performances were mediocre and I was at my most effective when batting out for a draw much to the annoyance of Sandra who invariably set off for home before the end of the match. It was a disappointing season for the team and only in the last game was relegation avoided. We had to win at Green Lane where we were asked to bat first. After 5 overs we had lost three wickets with no runs on the board. We recovered and near the end of our innings I hit a couple of boundaries to lift our score to just over a hundred. With not much to bowl at, we needed an early break through. In the first over the ball was struck back over the bowler's head and I ran round from mid on. On hearing the call of 'come for two' I turned and threw the ball in one quick movement straight to the bowler right above the stumps. The batsman was well out of his ground and didn't even bother to look at the umpire. After that wickets fell at regular intervals and what had seemed like mission impossible after the first five overs became a comfortable victory.

One other memory of the 1966 season was that Saturday in June when England won the World Cup; everyone wanted to watch the football match and some cricket leagues made arrangements for the games scheduled for that day to be played at a later date. The Airedale and Wharfedale League bucked the trend but never before was I so pleased when rain prevented any play at cricket. The game was called off and we didn't hang around.

1967 was another mediocre season for me with the only highlight being when I took six wickets against Illingworth on a bumpy pitch bowling seam up. The following year continued in the same vein and I volunteered to play in the second team as they were short of early order batsmen although I would not dispute the fact that I went before I was pushed.After a slow start which included being run out before I had received a ball at Addingham I had a successful season with the bat. In 11 innings with two not outs, I scored 261 runs for an average of 29.One of the highlights was my maiden half century which came in a match at Illingworth.I was on 44 when I hit a six over extra cover. The ball only just cleared the boundary but unlike my previous effort at Whitkirk, this one counted.

The main feature of my spell at Menston was my conversion from a bowler who batted a bit to an opening batsman who didn't bowl. With hindsight it was a mistake to give up bowling as in seven and a half seasons prior to 1966, ignoring two years National Service and a part season at Burley, I had taken over 120 wickets at Pudsey Britannia, Kirkstall Educational and Farsley. Not prolific but not insubstantial either.

CHAPTER 34

Playing Cricket 1969

In January 1969, I changed jobs and, dazzled by the doubling of my salary, went to STC, an American company in Harlow, Essex. I didn't get the job I had applied for but was so flattered when they offered me the same money on the premise that when something suitable came up I would get a permanent appointment. This turned out to be a huge mistake and by the end of June I was back 'up north'.

Sandra and the girls moved down in March and we rented a house in Old Harlow. On the sporting scene, I would watch Spurs and West Ham.

When the cricket season arrived I joined the company team and was made very welcome as were Sandra, Karen and Jane. The real bonus as far as Sandra was concerned was the Sports and Social club, particularly when the weather was inclement. On the field I did nothing spectacular. We drove down to North London for one match and my head was still spinning after coping with the volume of traffic and it was no surprise when I lasted only a few overs. In another game, the pitch at the picturesque ground at Theydon Bois was slow and bouncy and I played too early and was caught and bowled. However I did get a half century in a home game where the pitch was in good condition.

If the game finished early, a 'beer' match was organised. This entailed reversing the batting orders and each player had to bowl two overs in what was obviously a twenty over contest. I hesitated before including this little nugget of information in case the ECB hear about it and make the twenty/

twenty competition even more of a farce. The idea of a 'beer' match was that the losers bought the first round of drinks and for some players this concentrated the mind.

I got a job in York and after a short spell of living with my parents we moved to a flat which was handy for work. On Saturdays, we drove over to Menston who appreciated the extra body to ease the problem of regular players being on holiday. The only incident of note was a catch at slip off the bowling of Bill Brown at Bilton.

During the winter, one of my work colleagues, Les Dent, recommended that I play next season at Tadcaster who were in the First Division rather than the more local team at Bolton Percy who, at the time, appeared to be having problems with their ground.

CHAPTER 35

Tadcaster 1970 to 1972

Of the 1969 team, only Barry Firn had moved on and so, not surprisingly, I made my debut in the second eleven at Boroughbridge – no drama this time.

Our opening attack bowled out the home team for a low score and I did not get into bat. My contribution was to hold on to two catches. A fortnight later we were at Sheriff Hutton on that picturesque ground just below the castle and the only incident of note involving me was a superb run out – fortunately we were fielding. I was at mid wicket in a position where I was neither saving one nor four when a left hander pushed the ball on the leg side and called for an easy single which I could not prevent. Later in the over he played a shot identical to the one earlier and set off at an ambling pace. His partner saw that I had moved closer and shouted 'No'. It was too late for the leftie, a rather stout gentleman

Tadcaster CC 1969
B Wallis (Scorer) B Firn, C Benjamin, F Hardy, B Westerman, E Wallis, D Cornthwaite
C Mason, I Atkinson, D McKay, R Dowdall, T Downey

with a turning circle equivalent to an oil tanker. I had the ball in the 'keeper's hands in no time and he made his way back to the 'hutch'.

I had not done anything startling but found myself in the first team for most of the season after that. We were struggling and eventually relegated, but I recall a victory at Sessay where I added some quick runs at the end of innings and then our bowlers did their stuff and we had an unexpected win. At the time Sessay's ground was outside the village at the far side of the main East Coast railway line which entailed negotiating an unmanned level crossing at a point on the track where the trains often reached speeds of 100mph. Not a situation for the faint hearted.

In contrast we were outclassed at Northallerton, the champions that season, who had in their team a player called Johnson, who had had several games for Yorkshire. Possibly it was our woeful display which prompted them to move to the North Yorkshire and South Durham League. As sometimes happens with teams who are not successful, the spirit in the camp was low but we hoped that playing in a lower division next season would improve matters.

1971 was a disappointment for the first team finishing in 6th place well off a promotion place. Eric Wallis was the star. He topped the division batting averages and was fifth in the bowling. I was in and out of the first team but had quite a reasonable season with the bat. It must have been after one of my better performances in the first team that I was, much to my surprise, asked to captain the side; apparently the regular skipper was away as were the more likely replacements. The match was a local derby against Thorp Arch and Boston Spa. We won easily thanks to Eric who was determined to beat TABS on his own; he had a useful bowling spell and then carried his bat for an unbeaten 90 something in a 7 wicket victory. I neither batted nor bowled and didn't handle the bowling all that well. I thought Dave Cornthwaite could bowl through the TABS innings and had to make a change when he tired; fortunately it did not have any major effect. At the end of the day I hold the record (I think) as being the most successful skipper in the club's history with my 100 % record albeit in only one match.

My first memory of the 1972 season was a match at York Sugar when we were rained off; I had just taken guard. We rushed off the field and into the nearby social club to watch the FA Cup Final between a team from the south and that lot from LS11.Naively I thought we might return to the cricket field when the rain stopped but no one was watching the weather outside; I saw that wonderful header from Alan Clarke after Mick Jones had crossed from the right which won the Cup. It was an odd experience sitting in the social club with my pads on enjoying a soft drink appreciating what was a superb goal.

Although we did eventually resume playing cricket, the match was ruined by the weather and, with no chance of a result, the captains called it a day when the rain returned. One or two of us went to The Green Tree in Beckfield Lane at the suggestion of Tony Stead who had just re-joined the club. Tony strengthened the bowling attack and took 59 wickets at 9.66 and with David Cornthwaite second in the division averages with 40 wickets at 7.60 backed up as usual by Eric Wallis who got 50 victims, the bowling was in good hands. Our batting did not rely on Eric Wallis as there were contributions from Chuck Benjamin, Ray Dowdall, Fred Hardy and Terry Downey.

Promotion looked a distinct probability when we came to the last set of fixtures; Hovingham could not be caught and won the Division but we were in second spot with 67 points. Dringhouses had 66 points and Railway Institute, the outsiders with 65.The scoring system at the time was 5 points for a win, 3 for a 'winning' draw and 1 for a 'losing' draw. Our last match was at home to Dringhouses and so whoever won would get promotion. If the result was a draw and RI won, they would sneak in by the back door.

We had bowled our opponents out for 140 and at 65 for 3 and up with the run rate required on a good pitch with a fast outfield, our destiny was in our own hands. Then the saying in cricket that a couple of quick wickets can turn a game round proved to be true once again. With two new batsmen at the crease we struggled and when the next wicket fell we needed 50 runs to win in eight overs and six wickets were down.I strode to the crease knowing it was 'muck or nettles'. At the other end 3 wickets fell and Dringhouses were the favourites; however I managed to dominate the strike. Just as I can remember the best delivery I ever bowled some 26 years earlier, the best shot at batting came in this match. Peter Smales, an experienced bowler who always figured in the averages, was brought back on at the Leeds Road end and delivered a ball which was straight and just short of a length; I hit it on the rise back over his head. The ball never rose above six feet high and hit the sightscreen like a cannon shell. I am sure that if the sightscreen had not been there it would have been shuffling the dominoes at the Fox and Hounds on Leeds Road.

I was facing the last ball of the penultimate over with 12 runs required and stroked the ball towards a fielder on the boundary edge for a single so that I kept the strike when someone shouted to the youth who was about to pick up the ball 'Leave it'. He did and we had a boundary four but, more importantly, it left Barry Westerman to face the final over from Peter Smales. With nine wickets down we could not afford a suicidal single. Barry survived but could not score, with the result that we had 68 points and Dringhouses 69. I was left stranded at the non striking end 40 not out; from a personal viewpoint, it was disappointing that if I had got a few more runs I would have qualified for the league averages. Any personal feeling however, paled into insignificance compared with that of the entire team who was devastated.

It was the turn of Dringhouses to share our feelings when the news came in that RI had won their game and had 70 points to win promotion. Their victory was a tremendous effort as they had to play on the pitch of their opponents, Acomb, as the RI ground was not available.

During the winter I decided to retire at the age of 34 as I was disillusioned with the game. This enabled me to sort out my garden which had been neglected and was in urgent need of attention. I was able to watch the 1973 FA Cup Final – hard lines to the lads from LS11.

CHAPTER 36

Bolton Percy

I had not missed playing during 1973. After the following season had started, Gordon Bradley called round to see whether I would help him out. He was the skipper of the second team at Bolton Percy and was short of players. Gordon is very persuasive and I found myself looking into cupboards for my gear for an away fixture at New Earswick.

Gordon lost the toss and I found I was to open the batting; better to get it over with, I thought.

The ground at New Earswick is larger than most and is part of a sports complex which includes soccer, rugby league and tennis. The actual area is a vast open field where there is nowhere to hide from the elements. In this case it was a strong breeze which, no doubt, had emanated from Siberia. Despite the conditions, it was a case of returning to dramatic debuts. I was the ninth batsman out having scored 51 out of a total of 101 in the penultimate of our allotted overs. The bounce on the pitch was variable and the outfield very slow as the grass was long and the surface somewhat spongy. That is my excuse for a painstaking but invaluable innings. We lost the match by 2 wickets and I took three catches at cover point – all skiers from mishits.

Much to Gordon's chagrin, I was selected in the first team when I returned from holiday. Just as all those years ago at Pudsey Britannia, a debut success in the second team was followed by a good performance after promotion to the first eleven, this time with the bat rather than the ball. The opponents were Woodhouse Grange second team who batted first and scored just under

200. Whilst the pitch had variable bounce, unlike the previous week, the boundaries were short and the opinion in the dressing room at the interval was that the target was achievable. I went in to bat at number six when we were a little behind the run rate and was full of confidence after the previous knock. The runs flowed more freely and I had reached 60 when I mistimed a drive and was caught and bowled. We looked like winning but there was a sudden collapse and we lost by 4 runs. The season went well with the first team gaining promotion to Division 2.The final round of matches in the York area were all rained off but Nawton Grange whose ground was just outside Helmsley managed to complete their game and by winning it took the title. We ended up in second place just pipping our near rivals Bishopthorpe for the other promotion spot. On a personal note I scored 266 runs at an average of

Bolton Percy CC 1974
K Spittle, A Child, J Waterhouse, H Houseman, C Taylor, D Hall, Joe (?) Scorer, G Pears, D Bell, G Gibbs, M Wensley, I McKenzie

24.18.

Promotion to Division 2 was a bridge too far and we finished in bottom place. Following a match winning innings of 80 not out against Ripon I scored 254 runs at an average of 19.55. Back in Division 3 we just missed out on a quick return ending up in third place. I managed to notch 255 runs averaging 21.25.

It was on 16th July 1977 that I scored my maiden century against New Earswick. We batted first and lost wickets at regular intervals. I had gone in at number 3 and when I reached the half century mark realised I had to carry on batting normally as we were 90 for 6. Our tail was not known for its wagging qualities. Eventually I was ninth out for 106 in the penultimate over with the score on 190. Unfortunately we could not bowl our opponents out and got a bonus draw. We finished in mid table but I was pleased with my personal performance in scoring 416 runs at an average of 26 – I could have done with a few more not outs!

There was a remarkable batting performance from the Bolton Percy team at TABS.Put into bat, we lost a wicket in the first over and so I joined Mike Wensley. Our partnership came to an end 156 runs later. Mike scored 113 while my share was only 42, However when we perused the score book our scoring rates were more or less the same. I had not much of the strike and had scored in singles whereas Mike was hitting boundaries. Henry Houseman and Phil Lazenby then added 103 in quick time and we declared at 259 for 3 after 40 overs. Once again we could not dismiss the TABS tail enders and had to be content with a draw.

For the 1978 season I was elected captain. We finished in mid table in Division 3 but had some success in the cup competitions. In the Gilmour and Dean Trophy Sunday Knock Out we were drawn at home to Magnets on 25th June – a clash of dates with the World Cup final in Argentina. There was a spot of rain here and there and also a dodgy forecast. We all wanted to watch the football in the evening and as there no officially appointed umpires, I agreed with the Magnets skipper we would reduce the overs from 40 to 35. This was probably against the rules. Magnets raced to 215 for 3 in their allotted overs and we were up against it as, although the rain held off, the light was poor. I went in at number 6 to join Peter Lazenby knowing that we had not got a lot of batting in the 'hutch'. We were up with the run rate and needed a run per ball. The Magnets skipper decided to place the majority of his fielders to cover the short boundaries leaving plenty of scope for singles. Peter and I took singles if we could not beat the field but a boundary early in the over was a bonus. We saw our team home. Peter was 66 not out and I was unbeaten with 45, 27 of which were singles. Argentina won the World Cup with Mario Kempes, the long haired one, scoring a spectacular goal.

In the next round we drew Thorp Arch and Boston Spa (TABS) who in the previous round had beaten their fierce rivals Tadcaster. TABS were in a division higher and fancied their chances as they had home advantage. A couple of weeks before the match was to take place we signed up Steve Lawrence, son of the legendary Johnny who played for many years with Somerset. Unfortunately Steve was not eligible to play in the cup match and someone from the second team was drafted in. Consequently, I was very surprised to see him changed and having some practice on the outfield. It appeared that one of the regular players could not play and two of the selectors, unaware of the position regarding Steve, told him he could play. I was presented with a problem in that Steve was known to the TABS players and suggested to the rest of the team that we play with ten players. My idea met with a great deal of opposition, particularly from those who had mainly played friendly cricket previously. When I went to toss up with the TABS skipper, he asked if Steve was playing and was I aware of the rules of the competition. I knew the situation, of course, but we agreed to play the match on the basis that TABS would go through to the next round irrespective of the result.

Steve got a duck and only bowled three expensive overs. However Bolton Percy won the cricket match. As we came off the field, some of the Tadcaster players who had spent quite some time on the nearby Pax Inn, suggested to the TABS skipper that if they couldn't beat Bolton Percy, they didn't deserve to go through to the next round.Fortunately for us most of their team had been invited to a wedding reception on the evening before the date of the next round and, as some would say they got their priorities right. They accepted the result and we were in the quarter final against Woodhouse Grange, one of the stronger sides in the top division.

I lost the toss. Bolton Percy batted first and were scoring at the rate of 5 per over without losing a wicket when down came the rain. In no time the pitch was under water and play was abandoned. The rules stated that we then had to toss a coin to see who would go through. Woodhouse, wanting to avoid the lottery, suggested that we play a 20 over game the following evening. We agreed but when Woodhouse contacted the League they were told to stick to the rules. I met Alistair Swann, the opposing skipper, on the Monday tea-time in the car park at Hargreaves Fertilisers.I spun the coin and Alistair guessed correctly much to his relief. Our cup run was over in very disappointing circumstances.

The other cup competition we entered was the Harbord Trophy; most of the games were played at Tadcaster on an evening – probably to boost the bar takings. We reached the final and were asked to be at Tadcaster at 2pm on a Sunday afternoon. I struggled to get a team as most of our players had wives and families and we certainly had a much weakened team. On arrival we found that the other semi final was just starting and that the final was scheduled for 4.30. I had a mutiny on my hands and we almost decided to concede and go home. We all stayed apart from John Dale, our young wicket keeper who had said earlier that he had a family 'do' to attend at 5pm.One of our supporters was press ganged to make up the eleven. With a makeshift team, not in the best of spirits, and a 'volunteer' 'keeper we were certainly not the favourites. We lost to our old rivals, Cawood but were not disgraced. This incident confirmed my opinion that success in sport is mostly in the mind as that Sunday we knew we had no chance. Another cup run ended in unfortunate circumstances.

My personal performance in the season was disappointing and I am sure it was affected by the fact that I was the skipper and had also spent a great deal of time assisting David Green with preparing the square.

Another reason why I did not figure in the league averages was the excellent form of the other batsmen. Openers Roger Moir and Mike Wensley amassed almost 1000 runs between them while Henry Houseman chipped in with 256 and David Hall scored 231.

There was an amusing incident off the field. After the away match at Rowntrees, we gathered in the Punch Bowl (now the Independent) and as I was not driving, was enjoying the excellent bitter but on my return from 'turning the car round' found that the designated drivers had disappeared leaving Alwyn Anderson and myself behind. Clearly we had to make a decision as to what to do and so we ordered another pint. We had the choice of getting a taxi or touring the city centre pubs while waiting for the local village bus which set off from Skeldergate at 11pm. Choice? A no brainer really. The jovial driver, set off on time with a full bus load. Some passengers were standing and others couldn't.

As a story on its own I think it is pretty tame but it does lead on to an incident which apparently happened two weeks later. This was told to me at closing time in the Shoulder of Mutton one evening and I can't give my authentication of its truth but it is too good to leave out. It is 11pm and the driver is about to set off when a young woman leaps on to the bus. She had been running and was out of breath.

In fact, she was breathing rather heavily with the result that her ample breasts emphasised the tightness of the skimpy top she was almost wearing; it was as if two puppies were having a fight. The eyes of all passengers, even those who could barely stand, were fixed on the young lady who really was well stacked in the breast department.The men ogled while the ladies were envious. Gradually the fight between the puppies subsided and she paid her fare to the driver who with remarkable calmness (I am told) set off down Skeldergate. As the bus passed the Cock and Bottle, an appropriate name as the story unfolds, the young woman asked a mature lady whether she could have her seat as she (the young woman) was pregnant. 'Of course' came the reply. Before the bus had reached Bishopthorpe Road, some 300 yards away, and with the mature lady giving the younger one a thorough inspection, she asked 'How long have been pregnant my dear ?' The young lady looked at her watch and said 'Oh, about 40 minutes but doesn't it make you tired'

One of the characters in the team was Geoff Pears who for several seasons was skipper. Geoff was known as Mr Fix It; if you wanted any thing doing, the

Geoff Pears – Bolton Percy CC

saying was 'Ask Geoff Pears'.His main job as far as the cricket teams were concerned was landlord of the Crown Inn. The cricket club did not have a bar at the time. Geoff, as often as not, arrived late; the excuses varied from changing a keg of lager for his wife Angela to organising a shooting party. Someone else had to toss up and, of course, always made the wrong decision according to our missing skipper.. Towards the end of a season, the league brought the starting times forward by half an hour and a group of senior players decided to give Geoff the wrong date; as a result he arrived 25 minutes early – he also lost the toss that day.

From a performance point of view, 1979 was also a personal disappointment and I alternated between the first and second teams. The only match to remember was at local rivals Bishopthorpe when David Bell (54 not out) and I (35 not out) saw Bolton Percy home despite some aggressive bowling by Steve Allison who lived in Appleton Roebuck at the time.

Bolton Percy CC
Geoff Pears and David Bell

I was not enjoying my cricket and at the end of the season decided to hang up my boots.Cricket takes up two thirds of Saturday and I could spend my time doing other things. There was the excitement of the tennis club finding its feet in the leagues and also resurgence in the fortunes of Huddersfield Town.

A career which had started with such a bang when walking through the door in the Guinness advert in Hunslet had ended in a whimper 25 years later.

CHAPTER 37

Umpiring Cricket

My first experience of umpiring came towards the end of my playing career. Both Bolton Percy teams were in divisions of the York and District Cricket League where matches were not covered by the neutral panel of umpires and were obliged to provide a competent person to officiate. Quite a few teams, including BP, struggled to find someone and so it was the regular practice for two members of the batting side to don the white coats; there were frequent changes as wickets fell resulting in a lack of consistency. I didn't mind doing my stint and, after my presence at the crease had been terminated, would often do the rest of the innings.

About six years after I had finished playing, I was asked if I would join a small panel to umpire first team matches and I agreed. This arrangement only lasted one season as promotion to Division 2 was achieved. This was on account of the fact that they were a good team and not any undue influence by umpires. The panel of neutral umpires operated in Division 2.

I volunteered to stand for the second team in division 5.Sometimes the other club had an umpire but when they had not, I would take the bowler's end for the full 90 overs. This brings to mind an amusing incident when the skipper of our opponents requested that we indicate on the result sheet that his club had provided an umpire; someone agreed and gave the missing official 7 marks out of ten. However as our skipper was about to add his signature, he noticed that I had been awarded only 6 marks;after a few harsh words, not by me I might add, the figure was altered to 8.

In the last match of one season bad light and then rain forced us off the field and my colleague and I told the two captains we would look at the situation in 15 minutes. The match was evenly poised with both teams capable of winning; however the light had deteriorated with the rain getting heavier, we decided to abandon play. We found the two skippers at the bar already on their second pints.; 'Oh' they said ' we decided we had had enough – should we have told you ?' I was quite pleased they didn't want to play but what would Dickie Bird have had to say if he had been in charge?

Weather is often a contentious point. Rowntrees had racked up 189 for 1 in 27 overs when we left the field with thunder and lightning not far away; it was clear play would not resume for a while. We took an early tea and the 'Trees skipper declared his side's innings closed. The Bolton Percy skipper didn't want to play on the basis that his team would get more points if the match was abandoned and added that I, after all, was the Bolton Percy umpire. I ignored his comments, play resumed and in the remaining overs BP scored just over 100 for 4 thereby justifying the decision of myself and my colleague to wait for the weather to improve. The Secretary of the league was in the Rowntrees team that day and congratulated me on standing firm in the face of much provocation. Did I get 11 marks out of ten? Relations with the skipper remained frosty for several weeks.

It is not often that a team loses a match without losing any wickets but Dringhouses managed that feat. In their allotted overs they scored 216 -0 with both batsmen getting hundreds but Bolton Percy won in the last over by three wickets. The winning runs came from a straight six which not only cleared the boundary but St Helen's Road as well.

There was excitement off the field one very hot day at Cawood. I had noticed a young lady arrive, park her belongings by the side of her chair and sit next to the sightscreen at the far end from where I was standing As I walked to square leg after calling over, I glanced in her direction to see that she was undressing much to the amazement of everyone on the field; fortunately she had a bikini on. Clearly sunbathing rather than cricket was what she had in mind. After a couple of overs when long slender legs had been crossed several times, the batsmen indicated to the other umpire that she was a distraction. My colleague knew the girl and suggested to her that as the sightscreen would be moved shortly, she might find it more convenient to re-locate to a sunny spot just beyond the mid-wicket boundary. She did and the game continued. Needless to say several of the batting side decided to stroll round the boundary edge – as, of course, one does.

The club umpire for TABS (Thorpe Arch and Boston Spa) was Mike Rowlatt who in the winter was a Rotherham United supporter. Mike told me he was going to take the umpiring course and then, hopefully, to qualify as a fully fledged umpire. I had thought about this but the course in York was on a Sunday morning and clashed with tennis. However the Wetherby League held their meetings on a Tuesday evening and the instructor was Mike Eggleton, an umpire on the neutral panel for the York League; I really enjoyed these evenings and soon realised how little I knew about the game.

Everyone on the course got through part 1 of the examinations but part 2, where a 75% pass mark was required on more difficult questions, sorted us out Fortunately I scraped through with 76% paving the way for the final hurdle of an oral examination. I had to ring the Chief Examiner to agree a mutually agreeable time and place. I was told that the venue was Mirfield CC one Sunday at 11am – the examiner lived nearby. I was then asked whether I knew where Mirfield was.'Oh yes' I said 'I go near there on my way to watch Huddersfield Town'. His response was music to my ears when he said he followed Town – the omens were good. But what if he had had leanings towards that team who play 11 miles to the east along the A62?

On the day before the examination, Town were at home and so I did a small diversion so there would be no problems the following day, when the sun shone and I passed; the fact that I already was umpiring stood me in good stead. Town won as well – what a good weekend. I joined the neutral panel and the York Umpires Association.

The author in umpiring mode

The sequence of eventful debuts continued from playing to umpiring. My first appointment was at Clifton Alliance with Castleford the visitors in Division 2; both of these were their club's second teams. My colleague was John Clayton whom I had not met before. John said he was not going to stand any nonsense and set off to the player's dressing rooms where he very forcibly indicated that he would not tolerate any dissent or backchat; I stood there looking somewhat sheepish. The only player I knew was David Lord, the Castleford skipper, who didn't comment but merely raised his eyebrows. I had played at Tadcaster at the same time as David who, on his day, could argue with the best.

Castleford batted first and after the fall of a wicket which brought in a left hander I stood at square leg and for the first time was looking into the sun. I could not see the batting crease from 20 yards, the line was very narrow and the groundsman had been miserly with whitening powder. The Clifton skipper, John Bladen, came over and offered to have the lines re-marked at the drinks break which was imminent. It appeared that the man who came on to the field to do the necessary had not done the original markings and was quite jovial.

Castleford scored over 220 with a youth by the name of Bresnan getting 99 – I do not know which of the brothers it was. David Wainwright, now with Yorkshire, took over from his father Paul at my end but Clifton with a late flurry of quick runs won the game. The first apres match pint went down well and I thought I had earned it. Imagine my surprise when at the next umpires' meeting, John and I were told we had not to demand that the markings be renewed at the drinks break; our action was fully vindicated when the laws of cricket were revised in 2003.

As both Clifton Alliance teams were in the divisions covered by the neutral panel of umpires, I officiated there quite often and became a dab hand at climbing the vertical ladder to gain access to the changing room which also housed the electronic scoreboard; tact and understanding were the key words whenever there was a lady scorer.

During the latter half of the week, there had been a great deal of rain and although the covers had done a superb job as regards the actual pitch, the rest of the square was very wet; as my colleague and I went to the middle to do an inspection, water squelched up and there was no way play could start at the scheduled time. Most sides would have called it a day and not many games were played that day. However both skippers were very keen to play and the groundsman, not my jovial friend from the Castleford match, got to work with gusto. After almost half an hour of frantic effort, we reluctantly agreed to play Clifton won by three wickets in what turned out to be a good game; both sides used common sense in adapting to the conditions and thoroughly enjoyed their day. My colleague and I deserved to be in the Diplomatic Service that day.

There are occasions when an umpire exceeds his authority and I plead guilty; with the football and cricket seasons over-lapping in August, I had a clash of interests. I was standing at the pavilion end at Clifton and at 15.45 asked the fielder who was going to third man after being at mid on at my end, whether he would mind asking the lady in the green Vectra for the Huddersfield Town score. He gave me a rather odd look and so I repeated my request. Off he went and I saw him speak to Sandra who gave me the thumbs down sign. The youth returned to mid on and told me that Town were losing one -nil. His displeasure was very evident and the skipper came over to see what was happening; he was not too concerned and so I winked at him and then said to the young man ' Just remember, your side has yet to bat'

I was always pleased when I was appointed to officiate at Wilberfoss; their lady scorer worked in the club shop at York City and we generally had a pre-match chat about football. I am sure it was pure coincidence that in successive seasons I had their fixture against Beverley. Sandra came with me and I parked the car round the edge of the field so that she had a good view. She was concentrating on her knitting when Jamie Mitchell, the prolific Beverley batsman, hit the ball high in the air towards the long off boundary; I was at square leg and feared the worst. Sure enough the ball hit our car between the bonnet and the windscreen, bounced up and continued into the car park, eventually stopping at the tennis courts. My colleague signalled six and while someone was retrieving the ball I checked that Sandra was OK. Apparently she had heard a bump but carried on knitting. There was a small round dent on the bodywork just one inch from the windscreen on the passenger side. Jamie apologised but he hadn't done anything wrong. However when the ball hit his pads a few minutes later he looked up rather sharply wondering whether my decision would be influenced by what had happened just before. I turned down the appeal for LBW much to his relief – the ball was going down the leg side and would not have hit another set of stumps. Following that incident, I have never parked my car around a boundary edge since.

Tony Haines – Umpiring College

The following season I was standing at the same end and the bowler was the Wilberfoss star man, Andy Gray who went on to play for Yorkshire and Derbyshire; Jamie was the striker. An intended off spinner went down the leg side, hit the batsman's pad and that was the last I saw of it. The bails were off and Andy's whoop of delight was cut short when I called and signalled 'Dead Ball'. He made some comment about my eyesight as I went over to consult with my colleague at square leg, Tony Haines, who confirmed that the ball had hit the stumps direct and had not come off the wicketkeeper's pads. Jamie didn't argue and as I walked back to my position behind the stumps, Andy apologised and said 'Better to make sure ump' I was pleased I had got the decision right but thanked Tony for helping me out.

I must have been doing something right as I was appointed to umpire the Edward Readman Memorial Trophy Final in 2002 at Harrogate between Hornsea and Malton; my colleague was Dave Lockwood, an old adversary from New Earswick, who had skippered his club's side when I resurrected my career with Bolton Percy. The cricket itself was no problem but when we wanted to resume play after a break for rain. The groundsman was making things difficult and it took the intervention of the Harrogate Chairman to resolve the situation which was becoming very unpleasant. Some of the spectators who were unaware of the problem voiced their opinions in the direction of Dave and myself; the volume of the noise increased in proportion to the amount of beer being consumed. Fortunately the hubbub subsided when we got back on the field. Hornsea batted first but their total of around 150 never looked like causing Malton, or to give them their full name Malton and Old Malton, any problems and they won by ten wickets.

Bill Carter – Umpiring Colleague
This photoshoot interrupted Bill's preparation of a pitch for a junior match at Acomb CC

I got a phone call one evening towards the end of August asking me to umpire a cup final at Ossett on the Tuesday following the late Bank Holiday; this was a competition organised on behalf of the Lords Taverners for players less than 15 years of age representing the various leagues in the county. The final was between the Bradford League, the hot favourites, and the Airedale and Wharfedale Senior Cricket League and had been re-arranged due to bad weather on the originally scheduled date. My colleague was Bill Carter who had a black eye and some bruising on his face following an altercation with a cricket ball when keeping wicket a week or so before; Bill looked as if he had gone ten rounds in the boxing ring.

There was a huge crowd which ringed the ground – also several barbecues which sent out very appetising aromas. Aire/Wharfe batted first and were all out in the last of their allotted overs for 152; some of the more arrogant Bradford supporters were of the opinion that their openers would knock the runs off in no time. Their confidence was misplaced as by the end of the third over I had triggered them both LBW; the first came as a delivery jagged in from the off like a fast off break while the second never got off the ground. The fortunes of the teams ebbed and flowed and with ten overs to go, the match was poised. Having just given two run outs in an over, I thought we could do with the game slowing down and so I walked over to Bill for a chat. It then occurred to me that we had no guidance as to what would happen if the scores were level and Bradford had not lost all their wickets; Bill agreed to tell the players on the field why there was a delay while I went to find Phil Radcliffe, head of the organising committee. Phil realised what was afoot and said the emergency subcommittee had just decided that the match would be classed as a tie and that the trophy would be held by each side for six months. A quickly convened meeting if you ask me!

After I had given two more run out decisions, we got to the last ball of the match with Bradford wanting four runs to win – wickets of course were irrelevant. As the bowler started his run up, the noise from the crowd increased. I was concentrating on the area where the bowler's feet would land as the assembled throng turned up the volume The front foot was OK and I followed the ball on its way towards the stumps and the striker. It pitched on off and middle, moved slightly off the seam, clipped the bail and went on to the boundary. Most of the crowd thought the batsman had got an edge and that Bradford had snatched victory at the death. The upraised arms of the fielding side however told another story but it took quite a while for the more excitable supporters to comprehend what had happened. What a finish – who said cricket was boring!

Bill and I were presented with our mementoes first and I was delighted when we received very generous applause. Four run outs and two LBW decisions in a cup final – what a day!

With Australia taking on England in an Ashes series in 2009, the term 'sledging' comes to mind; for those not familiar with the term it means verbal abusing your opponents on the cricket field – nothing to do with playing in the snow.The Australians are well known for using this tactic which I think is a form of cheating. I have not found this a problem in local cricket where sometimes the comments are humorous. I recall a batsman struggling to hit the ball off the square inviting a comment from the fielder at cover point. 'This guy is going home on the bus – because he can't drive' That same fielder was later ordained as a vicar.

Before the start of each season I would ask Keith Houlston who did the umpires' appointments for a fixture at North Marine Road, Scarborough. On one occasion, the public address system was operating and I quite enjoyed hearing my name albeit there were only five spectators one of whom was Sandra. It was at Scarborough that I witnessed a death on the field of play. The bowler at my end sent down what he intended to be a cleverly flighted delivery but the batsman made it into a half volley which he struck with great force towards extra cover where a seagull was having a snack; the ball reached the boundary with a mass of feathers stopping some 10 yards short. One of the fielders picked up what was left of the seagull and we all stood, heads bowed, while he unceremoniously dumped the body in a litter bin.

The teas at North Marine Road were worth the journey alone but a late flurry of wickets almost caught the caterers out one Saturday. In addition to ham salad, they were providing new potatoes which needed a couple of minutes more. My colleague and I decided to extend the tea interval to cope with this minor crisis; both skippers were in agreement. Never mind league rules, let's get our priorities right.

The league operated a system of clubs giving umpires marks out of ten and while I never enquired about any individual match, I was interested in the average at the end of the season; usually I came out on or just above the average for all umpires and was generally quite pleased. There was an amusing incident at Goole when their skipper, Dave England, asked me what was the lowest mark he could give me without having to submit a special report. I muttered some expletive and he went away grinning; we both knew I had done quite well that particular match despite turning down several of his appeals for LBW. Dave bowled left arm round the wicket and, until the law was explained to him in detail by myself and my colleagues, expected to get a favourable decision when the ball struck the front foot of a batsman playing well forward with the ball pitching on middle stump.

Imagine his reaction when a batsman shouldered arms to a delivery which struck him on the pad just outside off stump and would have gone on to hit the timbers. 'How's that then ?' was the raucous appeal to which I responded in the affirmative raising my finger. He looked at me in amazement; I looked skywards and said ' There must be a god up there'

Another regular port of call was Sessay. In one rain affected match against Clifton Alliance my colleague and I got the weather right each time we were off and then back on the field, even incorporating an early tea with the co-operation of the ladies in charge of that important part of the operation. Clifton won a close match and both skippers made a point of thanking us for a good performance. Was it a case of eleven marks out of ten again?

As with Dave England, I got to know who could take a jocular comment, and at Sessay, Stephen Langstaff came into that category. He was also a left arm bowler and was introduced into the attack at my end at a time when the opening batsmen for the visitors were well set and starting to push the score along. His third delivery was a long hop which was despatched on the leg side; the fielder prevented the boundary and I was a little surprised when the batsmen attempted a third run. There was no reason to take a risk at that stage of the game. An accurate throw to the wicket keeper was too good for the batsman running to that end and my colleague raised his finger. At the end of the over when Stephen came for his cap, I said ' Do you always bowl for run outs?'. This brought a wry smile to his face.

In the next over the new batsman completely misjudged a full toss which struck him on the pad right in front of his middle stump; I think he just didn't pick up the flight of the ball. The embarrassed appeal was answered in the affirmative which brought another scathing comment from me at the end of the over. 'Never mind, Stephen,' I said ' Every ball that gets a wicket is a good one.'

It was ironic that it was at Sessay that I first experienced the problems which were later diagnosed as Parkinson's Disease. I had difficulty in concentrating and twice in the match with Beverley I signalled byes instead of leg byes. On each occasion I knew the ball had gone down the leg side but could not remember what had happened after the ball had left the bowler's arm. Fortunately my errors did not affect the score merely the reputation of the vociferous Beverley wicket keeper who let his feeling be known to all and sundry. None of the remaining matches in the season went the full distance but the decision to give up umpiring which was difficult at the time proved, unfortunately, to be correct.

CHAPTER 38

Tennis - The Early Days

While the game of tennis was accepted in our household, it was never taken seriously on the basis that my father thought it interfered with cricket. His theory was that in cricket, the aim is to keep the ball on the ground when batting to minimise the chance of being caught out whereas in tennis many shots involved hitting the ball up initially to ensure it went over the net. The conclusion, therefore, was that cricket and tennis did not mix and so tennis had to go. In the late 1940s it seemed that there was little interest locally and the courts in nearby Hainsworth Park were allowed to deteriorate.

When my brother Jim started wearing glasses he switched from cricket to tennis and as, his little brother, I was wheeled out to provide the opposition. We played in Westroyd Park which was four hundred yards from where we lived in New Street Farsley; there were two tarmac courts and one with a shale surface which we preferred in that the bounce was not as high and the ball came through quicker. When possible we booked the shale court for two hours but if other people wanted to play we reserved the court from 1pm to 2pm, played bowls for an hour and then resumed the game of tennis at 3pm. I generally won the first set – Jim had to encourage me – and then slumped to defeat in the next two sets which I put down to the fact that Jim is 6 years older. Jim became quite a good player as was his wife Avril and they played at Whitkirk for many years.

When I was working at Crompton Parkinson, I entered a competition and enjoyed it but did not take the game too seriously and persevered with cricket.

Many years later. In 1977, my interest in tennis was to be revived. During a meeting to discuss the arrangements for the Queen's Jubilee Day festivities it was suggested that there should be a permanent reminder of the occasion. Gordon Bradley, Headmaster at Appleton Roebuck Primary School prior to his promotion to a larger school in York the year before, proposed that the Jubilee Tennis Courts project be started and it was decided that he would lead a steering group of three with me and Tim Lumb.

The most convenient site was at the rear of the Shoulder of Mutton; Humphrey Smith, owner of the brewery (Sam Smiths) was approached and gave a provisional agreement for two courts to be built. Gordon, Tim and I went round Appleton and surrounding villages asking for £15 from each household on the basis that if the courts were not built they would get their money back. Sixty five people subscribed and with funds coming from other village community projects, together with the proceeds from tournaments organized by Liz and Brian Maunder on the court in their garden, the financial side of the project was progressing.

Planning permission was granted, funds from Selby District Council and the Sports Council obtained, a legal lease with the brewery agreed and building was completed in June 1979. Fifteen months hard work condensed into one sentence. I struck the first ball at 10am on 30th June 1979 and it was an ace; although I have to confess that my opponent was not the best player and I did serve with a following wind.

CHAPTER 39

Tennis – The Birth of a Club

After a series of friendly fixtures in 1980, a mixed doubles team was entered in the local league in 1981 and the first match at Heslington resulted in a narrow victory. It was a successful season with promotion being achieved. This prompted the decision to enter another team and within a few years there were four mixed doubles teams, two mens, two ladies teams and two junior sides.At one point in time, Liz Maunder looked after the boys while I was in charge of the girls; the logic behind this was that Karen and Jane made up 50% of the team with the remaining members of the team being Liz's two daughters. One of our fixtures was at an all girls school in York and as I sat near the courts I saw a rather worried little girl scurrying off into the school buildings emerging in a few seconds later with a teacher. On explaining why, as a mere man, I was on the premises of a girls' school and particularly the fact that my two daughters were playing, I was not only accepted as being bona fide but was offered a pot of tea and some sandwiches (no crusts of course). The teacher, an attractive lady as I recall, sat with me for quite a while and in modern parlance you could say I had pulled – just my luck, she was a nun in plain clothes.

There was an obligation for the mixed doubles teams with matches being played in the evening to provide refreshments and so when Steve Fila from the Diving School next door offered a steel container we accepted with alacrity. There were of course no windows and the door had to be propped open; it soon became known around the league as 'Railway Cuttings'. This was a temporary arrangement and in 1986, Steve re-claimed his container but offered us a small chalet which had been occupied as a home by a Mrs Whitaker. It looked rather quaint if fragile and was known as the Wendy House. In the spring of 1990 it perished in a violent storm. This meant we had no accommodation and had, reluctantly, to go straight into the pub after the match.

Efforts to get a permanent building were stepped up and in May 1991, Gordon Bradley opened the new clubhouse. This was after going through the procedures for planning permission, grants for finance and an extension of the lease and even though we had done this before, nevertheless it was a nerve- wracking time.

Equally difficult had been the building of a third court.It was not fair to use the Maunder's court other than on a temporary basis and a project to add another court, essential for evening matches, was initiated. After problems involving the lease, the re-location of a play area which the brewery had installed and the diversion of a Public Right of Way, eighteen months later, work was completed and for the 1983 season we had three courts.

Since their installation the courts have had to be resurfaced and repaired and the pavilion was extended to include toilets which we could not afford initially. As I walk past the club I think back to 1977 and feel proud that I, with many others, contributed to creating a superb village amenity.

CHAPTER 40

Tennis – Mixed Doubles in the League

I started life in the second team in 1982 and was very fortunate to be partnered with Marilyn Almgill. Not only was she (and still is she tells me) good at playing from the base line but was also effective at the net. In a match against Rowntree Park on their courts we comprehensively beat Richard and Rosie Cantrell who admitted afterwards they had no answer to our teamwork; whoever was at the back of the court drove the ball to a corner with the return being intercepted at the net by the other partner.

Marilyn Almgill

The format for the league matches was that three couples each played twelve games against each other making 108 in total; the winning team was the one with most games at the end of the match irrespective of how many individual rubbers were won or lost. We met Civil Service (their 4th team, I think) and did very well in the first round of games. The weather looked dodgy with black clouds approaching and so I urged our ladies to cut short their gossip so that we could get on with the game before the rain came. I thought I did this quite diplomatically but nevertheless received three frosty stares. The next round was just as good for us and we managed to keep the 'interval' as short as possible without any comment from our ladies. At the end of the match we won by 102 games to 6 which at the time we were told was a league record; the weather had improved during round two and three and I was asked what all the fuss was about.

We had another successful evening at Dunnington against their fifth team; Marilyn and I had won our first two rounds twelve love and were ten love up in the third. Would we achieve a maximum? Unfortunately for some inexplicable reason Marilyn lost her service game and we had to be content with 35 out of 36 games. For once my competitive spirit was curbed and I commiserated with her. Honest!

Marilyn Almgill holding the trophy for winning division 7 of the York and District Mixed Doubles Tennis League in 1982 with all the players who made an appearance that season

The second team worked its way up the divisions following the first team who always seemed to be runners up to Poppleton. After the departure of some first team players for various reasons, Marilyn and I were promoted where I realised we had to play a more aggressive game and go for more winners; it was no longer good enough to get the ball back and wait for an error. We did not win as many games but the standard of tennis was better. One evening at Riccall, we were involved in a relegation battle and a win was vital against opponents who had beaten us on our courts earlier in the season. We all played well and won by about eight games.

After a couple of seasons I accepted that I was not as effective and with some promising young players available, I stood down from the first team; I would probably have been dropped anyway. The selectors, in their wisdom or otherwise, put me in the third team but I soon found that opponents played on my partner who would not go to the net and I had not got sufficient fitness to counter this. I found this extremely frustrating and began to feel that the rush from work wasn't worthwhile.At the end of the season I retired from mixed doubles but helped out whenever there was a shortage of players.

CHAPTER 41

Tennis – Mens' Doubles in the League

In 1983 new ground was broken when a mens' doubles team was entered in the local league which at the time had three divisions. The league had been formed in 1980 with five clubs under the chairmanship of Derek Boorman of Dunnington TC whose company, Tyke Petroleum later became the league's sponsor. In 2009 there are 58 teams competing in 9 divisions. Promotion was achieved in successive seasons and so in 1985 we were playing against the top teams in the York area. The euphoria of success disappeared and within a couple of seasons we were back where we started in Division 3 – very much wiser and experienced.

Matches were played at 10am on Sunday mornings and with the same format as used in the mixed doubles, usually finished just after opening time when sorrows could be drowned or victories celebrated. There was one notable exception when we played at Selby where there were only two courts at the time. The last rubber was completed at around 1.30pm; the nearest pub was at Thorpe Willoughby and we only just got there before the 2pm closing time which meant ordering two drinks each. The landlord looked somewhat puzzled but fully understood when we explained. However we were not allowed another.

The yo-yo situation continued with promotion in 1987 followed by relegation the following year; this proved to be an absolute disaster as both mens teams were demoted. The situation was compounded by the fact that the Ladies' Doubles won the first Division of their competition. This was a magnificent performance and is unlikely to be repeated by any Appleton

Roebuck team.Having said that, didn't they let us know about it frequently or, ad nauseum, in my opinion? During the winter, following several games of fives and threes and the odd pint of bitter or four in the Shoulder of Mutton, I issued a Mission Statement to the male club members present. The gist of it was that we had to prepare better for the next season. I then followed this with a prediction that both mens teams would be promoted and the ladies team, the reigning champions, would be relegated. While I could influence what happened to the men I had no control over the ladies (who has ?); was it a gut feeling or wishful thinking affected by the excellent Old Brewery bitter?

Appleton Roebuck v Dunnington lead by captains John Waterhouse & Derek Boorman

After two warm up games and many practice sessions, both teams started the season well. Confidence and self belief grew and both teams won their divisions; the first team only lost one match out of twelve and the seconds only two out of ten. Meanwhile, our ladies were indeed relegated but with the highest number of points for a team suffering that fate. They won 5 and lost 7 and were unlucky. Needless to say we commiserated and offered shoulders to cry on. The success of the mens' teams was extremely satisfying for me personally as I had been appointed Secretary of the Tyke Petroleum Mens Doubles League in 1987, a position I held for 5 years.

The author with the tankard presented in recognition of five years service as Secretary of the Tyke Petroleum Mens Tennis League

One of the main duties of the league secretary was to arrange the fixtures; this was done in January for the forthcoming season and involved a great deal of work. There were 21 available Sundays and with most teams playing 14 matches, it would appear to be a doddle; however both Poppleton and Dunnington had three teams and most others two but any problems were overcome after many alterations from the first draft. There were some blank dates in the schedule but when one Appleton Roebuck member commented on the large gap between fixtures during July, he was told that was when the Waterhouse family was on holiday. A perk of the job I would say!

Appleton Roebuck and Poppleton – The author just in the picture far left

Matches against local rivals can generate excitement and a fixture with Copmanthorpe had some extra spice. They fancied their chances having won promotion the previous season and one of our former players, Roy Almgill, husband of my regular mixed doubles partner Marilyn, had moved from Appleton to join Copmanthorpe to get more regular league tennis. Roy was not in the Copmanthorpe team that day but came to watch along with Marilyn; I couldn't work out which team they were really supporting and I suspect they were not in agreement.

Our top pairing was John Giles and David Bradley.John was a slow starter and, as unofficial and non-elected captain, I suggested that John and David should play as couple number three with myself and Will Hanby, a young but very promising player, moving up to number one to take on the might of Alan Partington and Anthony Wales, a big hitting left hander, who were Copmanthorpe's leading pair. Will served superbly to win the first game and we then took Anthony's service game by taking the pace off the ball; two double faults didn't harm our cause either. Using his height to advantage Will intercepted at the net on three occasions and, with our tactic of slowing the pace on the ball working well, we won my service. Our opponent's confidence was in tatters and at the half way point we were 6-0 up. At this point Roy came round to ask what the score was; he could believe 6-0 but not who was winning. This info soon got to the other two matches and we won the first rubber comfortably. Anthony and Alan recovered and our score ended up at 9-3.

The next two rubbers were close but the damage had been done and the result was a win for Appleton Roebuck which was celebrated with our hosts in the Copmanthorpe Social Club where the odd pint or two slipped down the throat very easily. It was generally agreed that on the day we were the better team and we all looked forward to the return match at Appleton.

A combination of my advancing years and the progress of some of the younger players saw me in the second team but I continued to enjoy my tennis. I quite regularly partnered Sean Kilgallon who was devastating at the net but who would admit, grudgingly, that his backhand was not the strongest feature of his game. However his determination to win matched mine. The York branch of the Next Generation group had entered a team and we went to their courts where there was a carpet-like surface. This suited my game as the ball came through a bit quicker and did not bounce as high; in fact it was akin to playing on grass.

While it may have been an optical illusion, I thought there was a bit of a slope from one end to the other and as there was a stiffening breeze blowing 'downhill', it was decided I would serve from the top end. The pressure was on for me to win all my service games and with Sean's assistance at the net, I am pleased to say that I did. The first rubber was closely fought but we came out winning 8-4 but it was the second rubber that was to clinch our narrow and, to our opponents, unexpected victory. A young man, possibly of Oriental descent, missed an easy winner early on and muttered to himself; Sean, ever keen to exploit the psychological advantage made suitable comments from time to time and it was not long before our friend from the east completely lost his cool. We won 10-2 and held our own in the final rubber; with our other pairings doing well, the team scored a memorable triumph.

There was a very satisfying victory at Knaresborough who were pressing for promotion while we were in the customary relegation battle. We arrived at their courts which were on the site of King James Grammar School to be greeted by a full car park and a great deal of noise; apparently some religious group had hired a room there for their Sunday service. This was happy – clappy at full volume. They tried to enrol us into their 'movement' but we ignored them but one of our team members, Brian Jackson, decided to use the facilities at the school and they thought they had a convert. Brian, a Welshman from the valleys and no doubt a strong chapel background, managed to escape; we could not hear what he said but got the gist with the second word being 'off'.

As other games were played on the courts there were various lines in addition to those for tennis and, for the first few games this gave the home side an advantage. Both teams had their usual players and our opponents were confident as they had won comfortably in the match at Appleton earlier in the season. However, on the day, we all played superbly and won by a narrow margin. Brian, in particular was outstanding no doubt inspired by his flirtation with religion. The Knaresborough team were absolutely gob-smacked while, in high spirits, we boarded the team bus which also doubled up as a 4x4 vehicle owned by our skipper Pete Ziegler for his work as a farmer and surveyor. Pete had moved to Appleton Roebuck from Kirk Deighton and as we approached his former local on the way home announced that we all deserved a pint and he was paying. The landlord tried to persuade us to stay longer but we had to get back to the Roebuck to crow about our victory to the first team and also to have a few more celebratory drinks.

Another memorable victory came in the last match of one season when we had to beat Rowntrees on their own courts to secure promotion. After two rubbers the scores were level and I sensed that one of our couples on the adjoining court were struggling in the third and last rubber. Our match was hard fought and we were still on court when the others had finished. With the rest of the players looking on anxiously we got the last game receiving serve From the expression on the faces of our skipper, Pete Ziegler, I realised that situation was tight. The score was 30-40; our team were in a huddle and apparently all were agreed that if there was one man in the club they would want to be receiving serve it was JW. I didn't let them down. My return of serve was too good; all my opponent could do was to hit the ball into the net, although I had raced up the court to intercept anyway – well, I got there as quick as I could. Another celebration at the Roebuck.

A couple of seasons later, due to some administrative problems and a lack of communication, the second team were expelled from the league. Fortunately I was not involved as a former league secretary it would have been embarrassing.

CHAPTER 42

Appleton Roebuck Club Tournaments

From before the club was formed, Brian and Liz Maunder held tournaments on the court in their garden and indeed the proceeds from such events contributed to the cost of the construction of the two original courts. I recall an occasion when I had not qualified for the final but was asked to stand in for someone who had a dinner engagement and had to leave early. It was a mixed doubles event and Gerry Gregory, one of the 'proper' tennis players who had some experience of the game unlike most of us, was part of the opposition. I regret to say I do not know who the ladies were but my partner and I pulled off a shock victory. I began to think that possibly there was something in this game of tennis.

When the club had been established for a few years, a pattern of tournaments emerged. The first event of the year was the Men's Doubles Winter Trophy which took place in March and this was followed in April/May by a mixed doubles tournament for the Yorkshire Evening Press Cup. Next up was the Father's Day Men's Doubles in June and finally the mixed doubles tournament for the Denis Hudson Trophy in September. I have completed the grand slam in that at some time I have been part of the winning couple in all these competitions. One usually associates the term grand slam as winning trophies in the same season; my efforts spanned three decades and twenty one years.

There was no seeding in the draw for partners and before a ball was struck it was possible to predict the semi- finalists if not the eventual winners. I was lucky in 1983 to be drawn with Malcolm Blackwell in the Father's Day Men's Doubles and the following year with Marilyn Almgill in the Evening Press Cup; in both cases the favourites came up trumps. My next successes were in the Men's Doubles Winter Trophy in 1990 and 1995 with David Bradley as my partner. David was at least thirty years younger than me and, in the later match, it was agreed, or so I thought, that he would do most of the running around at the back of the court leaving me to intercept at the net. During one long rally somehow the roles became reversed and after David, a tall young man, had clinched the point with a terrific overhead smash, I gave him a quizzical look. He grinned and from then onwards dominated the match.

Judy Marriott

By 2004 I was semi retired from the game in that I was not playing in the club teams but decided to play in the tournaments. I had not had any success in the mid-season events and regarded the Denis Hudson Trophy as my swansong not realising the significance an unlikely victory may bring. Before the draw, on a coolish day, I would have settled for a partner of average ability and to finish half way up the group after which I could enjoy a couple of pints watching the semi finals and the final. Fate decreed that was not an option when out of the hat came the name of Judy Marriott, the number one lady player. The pressure was on – no lounging about with a pint glass in my hand. Our path to the final was reasonably smooth in that most of the best players were in the other half of the draw but we had to play over 50 games to get there. I was tired and Judy had a problem with her leg and we really needed a good start and a quick result. The final was to be played over a short set i.e. first to six games. Our opponents were Ian Illingworth, a fit individual and the holder of the Trophy, and Chris Howat, a member of the first mixed team.

Ian Illingworth

We realised we were up against it but raced into a four love lead; all was going according to plan. Ian and Chris then found their true form and won the next five games. I had to serve to stay in the game from the end behind which the crowd was assembled. I understand opinion was divided as to who they wanted to win in that although Judy and I got the sympathy vote it was getting colder. Fortunately we then had a slice of luck; the slight breeze stiffened and I won my service game quite comfortably which, of course, left Chris, in the deciding and final game of the competition, serving into the wind. At 30-40 and on her second serve, I hit my return into the corner of the court leaving Chris with a difficult shot which she put into the net Only after the second pint in the Shoulder of Mutton did I realise that the grand slam had been achieved.

Chris Howat

CHAPTER 43

Playing Tennis – Other Tournaments

The local equivalent of football's FA Cup was the Municipal tournament which was organised by a committee of tennis lovers who were prepared to give up some of their time. The person in charge of operations was a formidable lady, Flossie Slack who for her day job was the secretary for Sir Peter Shepherd. It seemed that each time I signed in to indicate that I had arrived, I complained at the draw; time after time in both mixed and mens doubles my partner and I were to meet the top seeds. To make matters worse, this meant an appearance on the court around which most of the spectators and other players were assembled. Not only were we thrashed but our humiliations were witnessed by friends and foes alike. In addition in the local paper we usually got a mention on the lines of the top seeds and had little trouble in the first round in beating John Waterhouse and partner 6-0, 6-1. I only got through to the second round once when with Roy Almgill defeated two young lads who took us to a tie break; I was the only one who knew the rules but we did win fair and square. True to form in the next round we were on the show court and lost to John Giles, who had moved from Appleton to Civil Service and his regular partner Simon Billington.

In view of the number of players over a certain age, the Committee introduced some new events and I entered the Veterans' Mens tournaments in both singles and doubles. On the Saturday I had a good contest with DaveTree who won a close match something like 6-3, 6-4. On the Sunday, I met Dave again this time partnering Malcolm Blackwell when the score was the same as on the previous day in another most enjoyable match. We played in splendid isolation on a court in Glen Gardens, Heworth without the pressure of appearing on the show court.

The next year Flossie did her usual and I was to meet the top seed John Linfoot in the first round of the singles albeit on an 'outside court' I had not been playing many singles matches and was under prepared whereas John had been officiating at Wimbledon and, apparently, had been practising with some of the professionals. Surprisingly, John started slowly and at 3-3 in the first set, I was still in the game but John asserted himself and won 6-3. Similarly, in the second set I was level at 2-2 before losing the next four games, although both my service games went to deuce. This was a cracking match played in the right spirit. John went on to win the trophy but no one took five games from him in the later rounds. If this had been cricket, according to the Duckworth Lewis Rules would have I been the runner up ?

Veterans' tennis was very popular and I entered a mixed doubles tournament to be played at Fulford; each player had to be over 45 years old but fortunately I knew that Marilyn did not qualify and avoided what could have been an embarrassing moment. I asked Terry Haw, the organiser, if he would fix me up and I met my partner, Christine Riley, as we went on to court for our first match. We lost and with that went our chances of appearing in the semi finals. Christine had a heavy cold and did well to continue and so we were both pleased with the way we had played in the remaining games in the tournament. Edith and Alf Bewick won the event for the umpteenth consecutive time.

While we were all enjoying a cup of tea after the final match, there was a request for a volunteer to stage the tournament the following year; I offered the Appleton Roebuck facilities, subject to committee approval which in due course was given. Liz and Brian Maunder offered the court in their garden so we had four available and Steven Fila again came up trumps by providing the power for brewing up. Sandra and a small sub -committee worked out who was doing what on the catering front. On the day the sun shone and the tennis went well. After winning our group, Christine and I qualified for the semi- finals where we met the holders of the trophy, unbeaten for years, if ever.

On number one court Christine and I played superbly and, with Edith and Alf, a bit below par, we won 6-3 – a memorable victory. However fate decreed that I had hoisted my own petard as the saying goes. With time getting on and entries for the competition somewhat slow. I had asked Malcolm Huntington, sports writer for the local newspaper and a former Wimbledon umpire, to give some publicity in his next article. This brought in the extra entries required including Malcolm's wife, Gina who had played at Wimbledon in her younger days. Her partner was Keith Turner, then aged 46 and a top player at York TC. No prizes for guessing who our opponents were in the final nor the result. We lost 6-1 and were lucky to get one. I overcame my disappointment and sank a couple of pints with Keith when Steven opened the bar in his diving club. It had been a superb day and one that put our club on the map in local tennis circles.

CHAPTER 44

Playing Tennis in Spain

On two occasions I have been asked to participate in matches while on holiday in Spain; neither was pre-arranged.

Our first choice of holiday, a wine tasting tour in France, was cancelled through lack of bookings and so we decided to have a sunshine holiday in Banalmadena which is just down the coast from Torremolinos. It was late September and the weather was still very good on the Costa del Sol. The crowds had disappeared and it was also cheaper than in high season.

We spent part of our time seeing places in the area and part on the excellent beach; we had got into the habit each afternoon of calling into the hotel bar on the way back from the beach to cool down and prevent de-hydration- the beer was not much stronger than water!.When our friendly barman Antonio had got our drinks he asked whether I played tennis; this surprised me but then realised I was wearing an old polo shirt which had the word 'Wimbledon' printed on it. I had bought it for 50p in a sale – tennis tops always come in handy. In no time I found myself agreeing to play on the court at the hotel next door at noon the following day; Antonio said this was the only time he could play due to his shifts as a barman but he would make all the arrangements including providing me with a racket.

The court was in a sun trap between the 20 storey hotels with a concrete surface. Whoever said only mad dogs and Englishmen went out in the mid -day sun had got it right; never mind the dogs I was certainly a mad Englishman. In view of the heat we restricted the knock up and Antonio, at least 20 years younger than me, served well and won the opening game easily; at this point I wondered what on earth I was doing there. I quickly got used to the pace of the court and found that while Antonio had a tremendous forehand, his backhand was weak and, as a small man, didn't seem to know what an overhead smash was. I took the first set 6-2 and was leading 3-0 in the second when I realised we had a spectator apart from Sandra who kept looking over the wall to check that I was still alive. The young Spaniard was cheering every time I won a point; Antonio told me he was his regular partner who was not good enough to give him a game! The guy's racket was OK though. Spurred on by my supporter I won the second set 6-0..

Antonio took defeat very well and suggested another match but fortunately we were flying home the next day. We went into the bar of the hotel and Antonio got the drinks in although I didn't see any money change hands. I stayed on for a while with Paulo, my supporter, and gave him some tips on how to beat his friend – payment was made in beer. Needless to say I had a late siesta before we went for our evening meal.

The next year Sandra and I went walking on a Ramblers' Holiday based in the picturesque white village of Competa which is high in the hills above the coastal town of Nerja in southern Spain. Our hotel, El Balcon, commanded magnificent views down a valley which went right down to the coast. The walking led by Mike, a Preston North End supporter was very good. The group of people on the holiday were all friendly and I found myself chatting one day to a young lady from Brighton who was a keen tennis player. I realised I should have known better but I am a sucker (no pun intended) for an attractive female with neat breasts and long legs who can talk about sport. The hotel court was booked for 4pm the following day when we had returned from our 8 mile walk. Sandra was not impressed in view of my exertions the previous year but at least we were not playing in the noon day heat.

Having rested for an hour I met my opponent at Reception to pick up our rackets and some tennis balls which clearly had seen better days. The surface of the court was tarmac with a few holes here and there. I remembered the wise words of Malcolm Huntington to whom reference was made in an earlier chapter when his advice in such playing conditions was not to let the ball bounce. Again, it took several games to spot the young lady's weakness, a non existent back hand. I needed all the help I could get as I was 25 years older. The score was 6-3, 6-3; the three games I lost in the second set were due to tiredness and lapses of concentration when I was admiring those long legs. We had not discussed what the stakes were and Emma offered to buy Sandra and me a bottle of wine but I thought that was pushing it and settled for a pint of orange by the swimming pool.

I was unbeaten on foreign soil but had sufficient common sense not to go for the hat-trick.

CHAPTER 45

Playing Tennis – The Indian Summer

When I retired from full time employment, I weighed up my options as to how to spend my leisure time. My brother was into bowls and there was the possibility of a mid-week membership at a nearby golf club. Sandra and I joined the Ramblers Association looking for some mid-week walking. However when Brian Maunder invited me to join his group of mature gentlemen tennis players for regular games on a Monday or Friday, I accepted at once; this meant I could get in some walking, play tennis and have weekends for watching football with Huddersfield Town or cricket at Headingley or in the local league; gardening would also fit into the general scheme of things.

Play commenced at 9.30am after a spin for partners and a brief knock up. By half past ten we had usually completed two sets at which point we all needed a rest; the bonus was that Brian then provided coffee and biscuits; I really appreciated this break for refreshments as my breakfast consisted of bowl of alleged healthy cereals and a cup of coffee which in later years was used to wash down a High Strength Glucosamine Sulphate tablet which, as far as I am aware, is not an illegal substance. After the world had been put to rights we played another two sets before returning home for lunch and a gentle nod in a comfortable chair.

Sometimes the biscuits were provided by David Hopton, a retired surgeon from Poppleton. David's wife Janet was honoured by being elected the Lord Mayor of York and this involved on occasions an overnight stay on a Sunday night at the Mansion House. This arrangement meant David could not call in

The Indian Summer – Brian Maunder, David Hopton, John Waterhouse, Roger O'Gram and Colin Robinson

at the local Spar shop in Poppleton for the usual packet of Shropshire Cookies and on one Monday arrived with a very fancy pack of biscuits. When asked about the change in routine David said he had got them from the shop on the corner – this was Betty's, the fashionable emporium selling coffee, cakes and all sorts of expensive delicacies. I suspect that the term 'shop on the corner' would not appear in their marketing campaign. David took his duties very seriously during Janet's term of office and, when he just failed to get to a ball he was asked, somewhat tongue in cheek, whether his chain of office had weighed him down; like a gentleman he took it all in good part and was overheard on a social occasion saying how much he enjoyed the badinage.

David had many contacts, particularly during his 'term of office' and one of these was Malcolm Huntington who had a grass court in his garden. We were invited to play there – what an experience!.The ball did not bounce as high and the surface was much kinder to the knees. Gina, Malcolm's wife, served lemonade when we had a break in play but the ultimate experience came right at the end when we had a tie-break situation. My colleagues, not as familiar with the procedure as me, were wondering what to do when Malcolm offered to act as umpire. Here were four geriatric players, not doing justice to a grass court, having the services of a Wimbledon umpire. I am pleased to say I won the decisive point with an ace down the middle.

We received a challenge from Alne TC to play in a match in November under the newly installed floodlights; this was to be followed by a Chinese meal at a local restaurant. Another great evening although we lost the tennis match. The following year we were invited again on what turned out to be a very foggy evening; imagine a yellow ball coming at speed out of the floodlit fog which was almost the same colour as the ball. We lost narrowly but nevertheless enjoyed a good night out – possible not for Brian Maunder who had volunteered to drive.

The Indian Summer – Quentin Howat, Robert Porter, Brian Maunder, John Waterhouse and Roger O'Gram

Another character was Robert Porter GP who was and, I think still is, the honorary doctor for York City Football Club;discussions on the problems at City and Huddersfield Town sometimes delayed the start of play. Bearing in mind the ages of the group of players, it was re-assuring to know that the medical profession was represented. Roger Ogram, a former Ombudsman and supporter of Tynedale RUFC played regularly as did Quentin Howat who for many years did sterling work for Appleton Roebuck TC..Colin Robinson who shouted 'Referee!' whenever luck went against him, also became a regular.

After five years of wonderful tennis, came the incident which was to end my career. I had not felt as mobile as usual for a few weeks but put this down to old age. David Hopton served to my forehand side and the top half of my body together with my racket arm moved to the right; however my feet remained rooted to the spot and I fell over. We completed the set, Brian and I were winning, and I played the following week but I knew something was wrong and on the advice of our medical duo arranged to see my GP, John Coop who is also a tennis player. A visit to a Consultant at York Hospital did not prove anything although I was given an appointment to see the Parkinson's nurse in January (2008). Robert Porter came round with a Christmas card and told me in his direct way that I had indeed got Parkinson's Disease. Robert knew I would want it that way and he was right.

My thanks to Brian, and Liz Maunder, for the opportunity to continue to play tennis and to make some more friends. You never know one fine Monday morning I may pop round at 10.30 – just in time for the coffee and biscuits, Shropshire Cookies or whatever.

CHAPTER 46

Watching Other Sports

Rugby League

In the late 1940s and early 1950s all professional sport took place on a Saturday afternoon. Sundays were still sacred and there were no live matches on television. This meant that I had the choice of Bradford City, Bradford Park Avenue, Huddersfield Town and Leeds United for soccer and in rugby league, Leeds, Bramley, Bradford Northern and Hunslet. If the situation was desperate I could go to Kirkstall to watch Headingley play rugby union.

Bramley's Barley Mow ground was the nearest but they struggled near the foot of the table; one match against Barrow, then one of the top sides, remains in my memory. The game started in a snow storm and Bramley, with the wind at their backs, led at half time after some sterling work by Kevin Cluderay in the forwards and a centre called Gibson whose long raking kicks repeatedly pushed Barrow back. The away supporters who had made the long journey were not worried; after all they had the Great Britain standoff, Willie Horne, and international wingers in Lewthwaite and Castle. But they had not reckoned with an act of God; the snow storm petered out during the interval and the gale force wind dropped. The pitch remained a mud bath and was not conducive to open rugby. Bramley tackled like demons and held on to get a narrow win although when Horne kicked a goal from the touchline just in front of where we were standing to bring his team within a converted try of the Bramley score, there was some concern for the home supporters. But the Villagers held on to record a famous victory.

Leeds were a much stronger side and their ground at Headingley was only a 4d bus ride away. After attending the wedding of a relative whose name escapes me, a group of us managed to sneak away to see Leeds take on Featherstone Rovers. It was a bitterly cold day but I was insulated by the number of glasses of sherry and port which had passed my lips; I was about 12 years old at the time. It was a tight game which Leeds won with the big Aussie centre Keith McLellan getting the decisive try late on at what is now the scoreboard end. The stars for Leeds at the time were Arthur Clues, Bert Cook and Ted Verrenkamp, all from 'Down Under'.

Bradford Northern's ground at Odsal was not as easy to get to from Farsley but was convenient for mid-week matches under the new floodlights if I went direct from school. One cup tie against the star studded Huddersfield attracted a crowd of over 60,000 but this figure was possibly doubled for the 1954 replayed Challenge Cup Final between Halifax and Warrington when the paying attendance was over102,000 but it was estimated that another 20,000 climbed over the fence at the far end of the ground. The police, realising the number of people involved, turned a blind eye. Warrington won a low scoring match with Gerry Helme having an outstanding game. On the way out after the final whistle, my feet didn't touch the ground for the last 60 yards to the gate as I was carried along with the tide of humanity. The queues for the buses to the city centre were unbelievable and it didn't take me long to walk and jog downhill to be in time for the last bus, number 90, from Hall Ings.

I had always wanted to go to Wembley and the only certain way was to go the Challenge Cup Final; I went in 1959, 1960 and 1961 and enjoyed the experience, particularly the try scored by Tom Van Vollenhoven for St Helens against Wigan in 1961.My latest visit was to the New Wembley in 2008 when Hull did better against St Helens than many thought they would. The stadium is very impressive but it did cost a lot of money.

Although I do not get to many matches now, I am a regular viewer on Sky Television where I think the coverage of the game is excellent.

Cricket

As I was involved in cricket as a player and umpire for many years, I have not seen a great deal of the professional game. My first visit to Headingley for a Test Match was in 1947 when England beat South Africa by 10 wickets. For the last days play my father got tickets for the balcony in the pavilion which was then the main hub of activity; the players' changing rooms were in the same building and I was able to get some autographs. The next year it was Don Bradman's Australians who provided the opposition and instead of the luxury of the balcony, I sat on the grass in front of the western terrace; by the end of the day, it was somewhat uncomfortable. On the first day the queue to get through the turnstiles at the Kirkstall Lane end, wound back down Kirkstall Lane and round the corner of the road opposite Queenswood Drive where the special buses which started from Stanningley and augmented the number 44 service, dropped us off. I saw the first two days when the contest was equal and was disappointed when England lost on the final day.

In 1949 Farsley had great run in the Priestley Cup when matches were not limited to overs per side but were timeless; it was no use bowling negative stuff, the batsmen had to be dismissed or concede through exhaustion. As I recall the first team to bat had to suspend its innings either after two and a half hours or scoring 150 runs; this was presumably to ensure that both sides had a chance to bat before the pitch deteriorated and also to attempt to restrict the time involved in completing the match.

Raymond Illingworth aged 16 in 1949 having scored 148 not out against Pudsey St Lawrence in the Preiestley Cup

In the first round Farsley defeated Bankfoot; Raymond Illingworth was top scorer with 41 supported by Tommy Walker (38) and Eric Leeming (33). Eddie Edwards with 4 wickets for 46 runs was the leading bowler.

Ray Illingworth 60 years later

The next round brought local rivals Pudsey St Lawrence to Red Lane. In an epic contest Farsley came out in top scoring 394 while Pudsey were all out for just under 300. The game started on the Saturday afternoon and finished on the Thursday evening.Shops closed early as the inhabitants of not only Farsley and Pudsey headed for Red Lane; there was not the distraction of Coronation Street. Arnold Hamer, who went on to play for Derbyshire for many years, scored 140 for Pudsey but according to the spectators at the bottom end of the ground, was run out before he had got off the mark; the Farsley supporters were irate while the visitors maintained a discreet silence which, in my opinion, said everything.

The key moment of the contest came with Farsley nine wickets down when my dad strode to the crease to join a 16 year old Raymond Illingworth who was 72 not out He went over to young Raymond and said ' Carry on batting lad, I will be at the other end'. Dad was eventually out for 39 caught off his glove at the tea room end while Raymond (he was not called Ray until he had played for Yorkshire) scored a magnificent 148 not out. That last wicket stand proved to be the difference between the teams. Pudsey resumed their innings but never looked like reaching their target; Dad took six wickets for 74 runs supported by Raymond who bowled 6.6 overs and had figures of 2 wickets for 31. I assume that it was the practice to have eight ball overs in those days.

Farsley CC 1949
T Walker, E Edwards, E Leeming, L Thorp, E Hargate, W Kaye, D Jones, D Bloodworth, D Waterhouse, R Illingworth, E Dowgill

Lightcliffe were the semi final opponents at Red Lane. Farsley topped the 200 mark and won by 70 runs. Eric Leeming was top scorer with 64, Eric Dowgill hit 60 and Raymond Illingworth supported them with 34. The chief wicket taker was Eddie Edwards 4 for 48 and AAH Phillips (a professional fast bowler from Leeds whose first name I think was Alan) took 3 for 11. The key moment of the game was the run out of Albert Hartley the Lightcliffe veteran all- rounder when he had scored 48. He played a ball down to third man and, possibly eyeing up the large crowd and working out his collection for a half century, was not content with an easy one but went for the two.

The second run was never on and Derek Bloodworth's accurate throw from the Stoney Royd corner meant he was out by a country mile. Albert did not look at the umpire and trudged off to the dressing room, bald head bowed, knowing that his error of judgement had cost his team any chance they might have had of victory.

Finals were always staged at Park Avenue which was a regular venue for Yorkshire; indeed a Test Trial was played there in 1951 when Jim Laker took 8 wickets for two runs. That day Dad sent me on ahead with the instruction to get some seats in line with the stumps. I thought I had done well but came in for criticism when Dad said we would not get a good view as gully, and the slips would be in the way. Fortunately Jim Laker soon came on at the Football Stand end and had a leg trap – well done son!!

Apparently the Bradford League Officials were disappointed that a club from the immediate Bradford area was not in the final but the players and supporters of Farsley and Yeadon cared not a hoot. Farsley scored just over 200 thanks to Eric Hargate (59) and Eric Dowgill (32) and with Yeadon losing their first 5 wickets with only 25 on the board, we were ecstatic. Eddie Edwards who was unplayable with the new ball, took four and Dad the other when, once again, the result of the match turned on one incident. Tom Falkingham was dropped at gully and went on to get 103 not out sharing in an unbroken stand of 180 with Jim Illingworth. Hearts were broken and, in my view, Farsley had snatched defeat from the jaws of victory with that dropped catch.

Farsley CC 1950
A Wilson (Treasurer) D Waterhouse, J Hastings, S Longbottom, R Illingworth, B Henry, A Clarke, A Hollings (Chairman) J Claughton, A Audsley, W Kay, L Thorpe, D Bloodworth

Yorkshire used to play the odd match at Harrogate. I took a couple of days holiday and went on the Sammy Ledgards bus which, conveniently diverted through Menston village on its way from Bradford to Harrogate. In a match where the playing time was curtailed due to bad weather, Yorkshire beat Gloucestershire by an innings and 67 runs. Ray Illingworth took most of the wickets with support from Don Wilson. One supporter could not restrain his feelings and, after the visitors had been routed in their second innings, demanded that they be put in again so that we could get our moneys worth-yes, he was a Yorkshireman!

In 1972 I realised that I had a claim to non-fame. My Dad, brother Jim and I were at Headingley for the Test Match against Australia and as the England skipper, Ray Illingworth, came on to the field to toss up, Dad commented that at one time he would be tossing the coin and then telling young Illingworth to get his pads on (for Farsley not England of course). Jim, to my surprise then added that he had captained the juniors at Farsley and had done the same; Jim is a year older than Ray. This left me as the odd one out – the only member of our family not to skipper a side containing Ray Illingworth; my mother didn't either but that doesn't count..

Another memorable day at Headingley was in 1977 when Geoff Boycott score his 100th hundred against Australia. He pushed a ball from Greg Chappell past the bowler and we were all willing it to reach the boundary in front of the Football stand; fortunately the ground had a pronounced slope and the chasing fielder had no chance. England went on to win by an innings.

When the issues regarding Geoff Boycott turned Yorkshire more into a debating society than a cricket club, I let my membership lapse and generally lost interest in first class cricket; I did re-join and, since retiring from my position at Portakabin at Christmas 2001, have made good use of my membership ticket. Apart from the championship -winning year, the cricket has been entertaining if not sensational, quite by chance, I have found myself sitting in a group of fellow enthusiasts. Sometimes the chat alone makes travelling to Headingley worthwhile.

At club level I have gone back to my roots and support Farsley in the Bradford League; in 2008 they bounced back from relegation the previous season to take the second division title. Sandra and I are Patrons and ball sponsors; we did not take much persuading when that effervescent character Eric Vevers got in touch. Yes, the same Eric Vevers who, with a little help from me, routed Gildersome in a Leeds League match 53 years ago when we were playing for Pudsey Britannia.. Another former Briton, Grenville Fletcher, can also be seen occasionally at Red Lane, the home of the Rams.

David Kemp, Brian Claughton and Peter Birkbeck

As at Headingley, there is also a 'parliament' whose members have a great deal of cricketing experience. The 'Speaker' is Brian Claughton, a former skipper who led Farsley to the first division title in 1962. One afternoon Brian was late and, after his excuse had been accepted, asked when the onions were to be planted just behind the boundary line. With the timing of a stand up comic he then said 'They will go with all the tripe you lot talk'. 'Other members of the parliament include David Kemp, a local farmer, Peter Birkbeck and Eric Vevers who produces the match day programme for Farsley Cricket Club.

Eric Vevers

On another occasion there was unanimous agreement that a bowling change was required at the Stoney Royd end and so Brian shouted to Robert 'Bozza' Thornton telling him to loosen up 'The skipper's' said nowt' came the reply but nevertheless he started swinging his arms about. Possibly he caught the eye of David Syers, the skipper, who asked him to take the next over. Bozza took a wicket with his third delivery; Brian sat back in his seat, folded his arms and smiled – another wicket for the 'parliament', nothing to do with the skipper or bowler!.

Farsley have strengthened their squad and hopefully will do well in the 2009 season which, at the time of writing, starts in a few weeks.

Horse Racing

At the time one advantage of using the services of two firms of solicitors was that I got invited to two lots of 'jollies' – days out to the uninitiated. Dibb Lupton, as they were then known, also had a partner who was interested in racing. Ripon was the venue and I opted to join the coach which left their Leeds office late morning; I also made what proved to be the right decision and travelled to Leeds by train.

We had a box where a light lunch was served; it was not a liquid lunch but it was not far off. For the first race I used the Tote as there was one of their selling points just outside the door to our box – how convenient. I picked a winner and decided to use that facility the rest of the afternoon; that was a mistake as it meant that I didn't get any fresh air. Still, I knew I could drink white wine for England – or so I thought. I had hardly noticed the waitress who had served our lunch but as the afternoon wore on and the white wine flowed, she became more and more beautiful but did I heed the warning signs? No.

I picked what was a sure fire winner for the last race; the certainty of all certainties and it duly romped home at a good price. Unfortunately I could not find my ticket but was not too concerned as I could collect my winnings some other time. On the return journey I, along with several others, fell asleep but woke up just as the coach got back to Leeds. I managed a coffee at the station before getting on the right train and telephoned home for Sandra to come and pick me up on arriving at York. On the journey back home, going round the double bend by Greenley's duck pond, it was alleged that I almost rolled out of my seat; I was not in a fit state to deny it!

During the evening, when I was more coherent, I commented to Sandra that I couldn't find my betting ticket for the last race – it was worth about £12. She searched my pockets, without success; at this point I had to confess that I didn't remember actually going to the Tote as I was having a discussion with a chap in the next box about football. Not one of my better days.

The other firm was Thomas Higgins and Co based in Wallasey. Tom's father had been a bookie and so racing was in his blood. Sandra and I were invited to Haydock with an over night stay at the Thistle Hotel. Tom picked us up in a gold Rolls Royce and for lunch we had champagne with some food as an afterthought. Champers was forced on us all afternoon and it was a relief when racing was over. We made a pot of tea back at the hotel and later noticed that Tom had left us a present – a large bottle of champagne. Needless to say we brought it home.

General

I have never had any interest in hockey, ice or field, and one visit to see speedway and stock car racing at Odsal was enough. Athletics does not appeal to me nor does boxing, following the greyhounds or bowls. I cannot recall any other sports but I am always willing to give anything a go.

CHAPTER 47

Time Added On

The fourth official has indicated there is time for a minimum of two more stories; regular attendees at football matches will be familiar with announcements regarding additional time just before 45 and 90 minutes. When your team is winning 1 minute is fine and if they are losing there must be at least 5 more minutes.

The first story is one which Malcolm Lord, who, in my opinion, is the best Master of Ceremonies for a sporting function I have seen and heard, tells against himself. When he was a young inexperienced reporter for the BBC in Manchester, he was sent to Station Road Swinton to cover a rugby league match on 11th November; the year is irrelevant. Although he reported on other sports, rugby league was his forte. He prided himself not only on his knowledge of the game but also on his ability to set the

Malcolm Lord (second from the right) with guests

scene for the listening audience and to keep to his allotted time span each time he was on air for a periodical update.

He was coming to the end of his three minute slot when he said ‘Oh, they are having a one minute’s silence. Someone must have died; when you come back to me, I will let you know who it is’. The response from the producer in the studio was on the lines of: You bloody fool, thousands died, don’t you know it’s Remembrance Sunday.?’ He continued for quite a while with the expletives coming thick and fast. Malcolm had to grovel and apologise as the BBC studio was inundated with telephone calls from listeners appalled at the insensitivity of that ignorant reporter at Swinton. Malcolm is a survivor and he survived on this occasion.

Dave Bassett (second from left) with sporting club members,
Jack Farrar and Don McEvoy

I have been to many sporting functions over the years and have guffawed at the humorous stories told by some of the top after dinner speakers in the land; but the following day I can remember none of them. I understand I am not alone in having this kind of amnesia which is possibly caused by over indulgence in falling down liquid. However one exception is the classic related by Dave Bassett who, although he has managed several other clubs, will always be remembered by me for his years at Bramall Lane with Sheffield United. When reading this, could you please imagine Dave telling this with his cockney twang.

Dave received a phone call from a friend, the manager of another club who were struggling. Their forwards couldn’t buy a goal and the defence had more holes than a sieve. It was a desperate plea for help. Ever to assist a mate, Dave suggested that a match be arranged between his team and a set of dustbins placed on the field of play in a 4-5-1 defensive formation. This should enable his defence to keep a clean (no pun intended) sheet while his forwards could bang in lots of goals against a static defence. What a great idea!

The following morning Dave got a call from his mate and asked how the match was going. 'Disastrous' came the reply ' the bins are winning 2-0 at half time'.

The final story comes from Paul Fletcher MBE who recalls an incident when he was a young footballer trying to earn a little extra money. One afternoon he and a mate were helping out a friend who had a business fitting gas fires and they arrived at the home of an old lady who was just setting out to do some shopping. They noticed a whiff of gas but were not too concerned until they saw a budgerigar lying prone in its cage clearly no longer of this world.

Another goal-bound header from Burnley centre forward Paul Fletcher

While the others installed the new gas fire, Paul was sent to buy a replacement bird having made a mental note of the size and colour. When the old lady returned, the new gas fire was working and she was full of praise for their efforts. Then she noticed the budgerigar 'Oh ' she said 'he has been lying in his cage for two days and I thought he had died'.

Most Sundays Sandra cooks a roast lunch with Yorkshire puddings as a starter while I go to the Roebuck Inn for a couple of pints of Sam Smith's bitter with instructions ringing in my ears that lunch is served at 1.30. Any time after 1.15 I say, without fail I am told, 'Sorry guys, it's time to go, the Yorkshires are rising' But what's this I hear. Is it the dulcet tones of my bride saying that lunch is ready; the Yorkshires have risen – sorry I that's all for now!

Paul Fletcher MBE

Epilogue

As the Ancient Romans said 'Quo Vadis' – whither goest thou? In this particular context what am I to do next. On the recommendation of the staff at York hospital I have decided to take medication in an attempt to halt the effects of Parkinsons Disease; I am told this could bring about an improvement in the co-ordination between my brain and my legs although I should hold back on signing a contract to be a professional tap dancer.

This treatment together with physiotherapy sessions has been successful in certain instances in the past and possibly that tennis racket might yet come back out of the cupboard. The answer is hard work and a belief that my situation will improve.

Realistically my active participation in sport is over; however it is now more important that in the summer I can watch Farsley CC, Bolton Percy CC and Yorkshire CCC playing attractive cricket and being successful while in the winter months hopefully Tadcaster Albion and York City will improve following mediocre seasons last year.

As for Huddersfield Town, I leave you with the following version of a song made popular by Mary Hopkin what seems like many years ago;

Those were the days, my friend.
We thought they'd never end.
We won the league three times in a row.
We won the FA Cup and now we're going up.
Oh yes, oh yes we are the Town
Oh yes. oh yes we are the Town

Come on you Blues!

About the Author

John Waterhouse was born in Farsley, Leeds on 13th April 1938 and was brought up in a sporting household as his father, Donald Waterhouse, was for many years a successful player in the semi-professional Bradford Cricket League taking over 1000 wickets. John inherited a sufficient amount of natural ability so as to be able to reach a standard in most games where he could compete as a reasonable level without ever getting anywhere near professional status. As a cricketer he made one century and on two occasions took seven wickets in an innings.

Having played Rugby Union at Bradford Grammar School, John missed out on those vital formative years of his development as a footballer and never caught up; natural ability had to be compensated by an astute brain and an energetic approach to the game. At the age of 26 he married Sandra and they bought a house in Menston; the journey on public transport to Farnley where he was enjoying football was too far so John hung up his boots to train as a referee. All was going well until a dissenting full back suggested that a visit to the optician may be beneficial – maybe he did not use those words but John got the message and from then on was advised to wear glasses. This limited promotion prospects and coupled with the return of Huddersfield Town to their rightful place in the top echelon of English football, he decided to end his refereeing career.

John left school at 16 years old and worked for Midland Bank. After National Service he moved to gain experience and had spells at Crompton Parkinson, where he met Sandra, Flexicon of Bradford and Standard Telephones and Cables in Harlow. The family returned to God's own county after only 6 months; the job had not worked out and John missed watching Town. Arsenal, Spurs and West Ham did not have the same appeal. Elder daughter Karen was about to start school and this also influenced the decision.

John and Sandra have lived in Appleton Roebuck near York since January 1970 and his sporting interests broadened. Golf and badminton provided enjoyment but had to go when family commitments – mainly two daughters needing transport for various activities. However tennis came to the fore and John was one of the leading lights in getting Appleton Roebuck Tennis Club 'off the ground.'

On retiring from full time employment John joined Ramblers Association taking an interest in public rights of way as a Footpath Officer. This led to the publication of a book of walks around Appleton Roebuck which he co-wrote with his next door neighbour Marjorie Harrison, a local historian and a successful author.

John fell over on the tennis court and was diagnosed as having Parkinson's Disease in Janury 2008, his active participation in sport and walking came to an end. With time on his hands he decided to jot down a few notes which led to the publication of his first book 'Memories of a Sporting Man.'

John is on medication to combat Parkinson's but can still drive although Sandra does most of the driving, particularly to Huddersfield. He uses public transport to get to Headingley to watch cricket and can managed to walk to the village pub and work in his vegetable garden.

He is grateful to the staff in the Neurosciences Department of York Hospital and to the Parkinson's Disease Society to who any profit on this publication will be donated.